PUSH

Perseverance Unleashed, Strength Harnessed

This is the story of unleashing the power within in order to persevere.
Of harnessing emotional, physical, and spiritual strength to survive.
This is one woman's story of her push to find hope.
This is *my* story...

Brooke A. Simmons

ISBN-10: 0615579701
ISBN-13: 978-0615579702 (2Peas Press)

DEDICATION

To Addison and Allison:

Your smiles have brought me joy in the darkest hours.

You *are* my greatest blessing.

CONTENTS

ACKNOWLEDGMENTS

I must first thank my mother who was also a young widow, and who can understand the painful struggle to rebuild a life for yourself as only another widow can. Without her unwavering love, support, and devotion I would be nothing.

To Keith and Teresa who bequeathed to me their son, whom I loved with all my heart while I had him, thank you for loving me like a daughter then...and still.

To Shannon, my best friend and unconditional supporter. Thank you for loving me like a sister, being there like a friend, and listening like a therapist.

To my blog followers and the other widow bloggers whom I have followed, thank you for welcoming me into the club none of us wants to be in and for making me feel heard. You've been instrumental to my healing.

To the countless friends and family members who have prayed for me, cried for me, cheered for me, and loved me through this process. You all are the reason I am still standing. Especially to Jennifer, your belief in this project truly humbles me. I thank you all for giving me strength when I couldn't find it within.

And of course, to Andie...thank you for loving me as purely and as truly as only you could. You are the reason for it all...

THE BACK STORY

Where it all began...

This was a blog that was originally created when life threw me the first curve ball...I found out I was going to have twins. That was surprising enough all by itself, but the really crazy part was that I wasn't even sure having one baby would be safe for me, let alone two. Let me explain.

I have a congenital heart condition that results in my aorta stretching and dilating over time. This can be exacerbated by an increase in blood pressure and I would run the risk of an aortic aneurysm or dissection; something that is almost always fatal. I've known about this condition since I was 15 years old when we discovered after my father's unexpected and sudden death that he had the same condition. Doctors told me for years that becoming pregnant was ill-advised and would be very dangerous due to the increased blood flow and pressure that occurs while one is pregnant.

After consulting with many specialists and a wonderful cardiologist who felt like pregnancy would be high-risk but not necessarily life threatening, my husband and I decided to give it a try. We knew we were rolling the dice but it was a chance we were willing to take after much discussion, prayer, tears, and heartache. I became pregnant the first month I got off birth control. We were elated and took it as a sign that we were supposed to be parents. A few weeks into the pregnancy we discovered it was an ectopic pregnancy that would have to be terminated in order to save my fallopian tube, and my life. Unfortunately, I hemorrhaged internally and had to have emergency surgery. The doctors miraculously saved my life and my fallopian tube, but our hopes were dashed. Perhaps it was a sign that pregnancy was too dangerous and this was God's way of letting us know not to go down this road again.

After more thought, prayer, tears, and heartache, we decided we would try one more time to become pregnant. If it didn't work we would consider adopting. If it did work, we were sure that this was God's grace. I got pregnant the first time we were able to try again. We thought it was a miracle as the doctor had told us to expect to have to try for several months to a year after just having had an ectopic pregnancy.

Everything was going along without a hitch until I went in for my 9 week sonogram. They were monitoring me very closely and very often to make sure I did not develop another ectopic pregnancy. At the 9 week sonogram they discovered I would be having twins. This was scary news to someone who was going to have a difficult pregnancy with one baby. Having two upped the ante significantly.

I started this blog then because so many family and friends wanted updates on how I and the babies were doing. Blessedly, I got through the entire pregnancy without a single complication and gave birth to two beautiful, healthy girls on August 4, 2009.

Life was going great! My husband and I had a solid marriage. We had two beautiful children. We bought land to build our dream house on. We had great, steady jobs, and lots of supportive friends and family members. We had the world at our fingertips.

That all came crashing down in June of 2010. Life threw me another curve ball, and although I ducked the first one, this one hit me smack dab in the middle of the forehead. I never saw it coming...

On June 18, 2010, two days before his first Father's Day my husband died right next to me in bed. He was only 34 years old. I was 29, and our twins were just 10 months old. My seemingly healthy, young, husband died of an old man's disease: atherosclerosis. The clogging of the arteries that is seen in much older men who eat really poor diets their whole lives. There was a combination of genetic predisposition and some bad lifestyle habits that led to my husband's death. He was only about 15 pounds overweight and exercised more days than not. He looked healthy. He acted healthy. He didn't smoke, rarely drank, and generally ate pretty decently.

I was left alone, bewildered, and reeling from shock. The blog became my catharsis for dealing with my grief journey. I had to find a way to continue living for my girls.

I used the blog as my therapy- a way to bear witness to all that had happened, all I had been through, and all I would have to endure. I pushed myself to confront my true emotions, process them, and accept them for what they are.

This book is a compilation of my blog posts through the first year and a half of my grief. It is mostly raw and unedited. Preserved in the original format to maintain the authenticity of my emotions at the time the posts were written.

Ultimately, this is a story about my push to find hope.

{PART ONE}

LOST...

The Lord is near to the brokenhearted and saves the crushed in spirit.
Psalm 34:18 ESV

Sun Sep 5, 2010 | 03:23 PM |
It's been a while...

So it's been a while since my last post. You've probably noticed a lot has changed on my blog. Well, that's because a lot has changed in my life. Andie passed away on June 18, 2010 and left me with two beautiful daughters to raise. It's taken me a few months to feel like I have my feet back on the ground and even that seems only momentary.

I considered not blogging anymore but have decided that it's a good way for everyone to keep up with how I and the girls are doing- I know you're all wondering. Raising twins is hard, but raising twins as a single parent is TOUGH, and humbling.

I've learned a lot about myself in the past few months. I've had to ask for help more than I'm comfortable with, I've had to compromise on a lot of things, and I've had to adjust my life plan. I've learned that I have more love and support than I ever knew was possible, but I've also learned that all of that seems inconsequential when you've lost your other half. I've learned that grieving for your spouse is just a small piece of the picture. You also grieve the loss of who you were as a wife, the loss of your hopes and dreams, the loss of the future you had planned, and most of all you grieve for your children and how they will never know and experience their dad as you did.

People often ask how I am doing. The truth is: it depends on the moment, the day, the hour, what song is on the radio, what street I'm driving on, or who's asking. I'm doing as well as I can with what I've been given. My girls are my saving grace and keep me looking forward to the next moment, day, or hour...

Sat Sep 18, 2010 | 03:54 PM |

3 months...

Today is 3 months that Andie has been gone and though it sounds like a short time, it feels like an eternity. The shock is wearing off and I've had a lot more emotional days, especially this past week. I know it will get harder before it gets easier and that pretty much sucks!

The girls are doing so well, they are 32" tall and got to move to big girl car seats facing forward this week! They are so proud of themselves! Addie is very close to walking and she stood up unassisted and stayed standing without holding onto anything for the first time today! They are both talking up a storm. They say, "mama", "dada", "ba-ba"(for bottle) and "bye-bye". They can sign "more" and Addie will sometimes say "nigh-nigh" for night-night. Addie also got her first haircut this week- it was really just a snip of a few stray hairs but that still counts right?!

I'm so sad that Andie is missing out on all of this fun stuff with the girls. People tell me all the time that he can still see them from heaven and I think if I hear that one more time I might scream. I know people are trying to be comforting, but it brings no comfort to me or the girls to not be able to experience things with their dad. It's simply not the same without him physically present.

We'll check in again next week and let you all know how we're doing. Hopefully things will be going a little smoother...

Tue Sep 21, 2010 | 02:13 PM |

Today, I choose to be grateful....

Today I choose to be grateful for my beautiful children and their heartwarming giggles! I recently have been feeling very sorry for myself and my girls, that they will grow up without their Daddy here. But today I am choosing to be grateful that they got to know him and love him while he was here. When they crawl over to the table where I keep his picture in the living room and pull up to look at it and wave or blow kisses to him, I feel blessed that they remember him and have a connection to him. It pulls at my heartstrings to see them wave and blow kisses at a picture, but at the same time I am grateful that they know who it is in the picture and want to connect with him.

So what changed my outlook you wonder?!?! Well....
I heard on the news yesterday about a preemie in the NICU in Australia. Everyday her parents drove an hour each way to visit her in the NICU- they did this twice a day to see their baby girl. On the way home a few days ago they were in a car accident and both parents were killed. It jolted me back to reality to realize that this poor little girl will never know either of her parents or remember anything about them- she is only 13 days old. My girls at least had enough time with their Daddy to know who he is and to have built a bond with him. They also still have one parent left, which means I need to get in the game and quit feeling sorry for myself. They need an active, involved, in-the-moment mommy who can teach them all about their daddy.

My commitment to my beautiful children is to be present with them, relishing the gift of time that we have together, bonding with them as often as I can and not merely going through the daily motions of being a parent. It's easy to get stuck in the ruts and routines of life and not really be in the here and now- I'm challenging myself to find a way to be more present with my children.

Grief comes in waves and cycles, and today is a good day. Tomorrow may not hold the same fortune. I am learning to take the good moments as they come and savor them. I have many blessings, so today I *choose* to be grateful.

Mon Sep 27, 2010 | 11:48 AM |
100 days, and 100 nights...

Yesterday was the 100th day without Andie. It's getting harder not easier, I feel crazier not saner, and so it goes... A book I'm reading says that grief doesn't come in stages; it comes in waves and cycles. I have to wholeheartedly agree.

You go up and down within an emotion and then move through it, and just when you think you're alright you cycle back around and start all over again. Shock, denial, anger, depression, acceptance- the 5 stages of grief...yet I manage to hit them all at least once a day, sometimes more. Sometimes I move through very quickly and other times I wallow in it. I cry almost every morning and every night but somehow manage to push through the day.

"Push" is my new mantra- I have to push myself to keep going, I have to push through the tough times, I can push through it all one moment at a time...I *will* push through it.

Mon Oct 4, 2010 | 11:45 AM |
Ten-Four

Today is our 7th wedding anniversary. Technically we only made it 6 years, 8 months, and 14 days but I'm still celebrating today. I went to visit Andie's grave early this morning before work- it was the perfect kind of morning that he would have loved. Clear skies, beautiful sunrise, and cool weather. I talked to him a bit and thanked him for choosing me as the one he wanted to spend forever with. I let him know that I was so complete and fulfilled with him and he will forever hold my heart. He was all I ever needed.

He gave me a gift that very few people get to experience in this world. The gift of complete, unwavering, true love. His dedication to me and our marriage was solid, and even when I look back at times in our marriage where I had doubts, he *never* did. I am so grateful for the time I had with him, though wistful that it could have been longer. This quote recently inspired me...

"Being loved deeply by someone gives you strength, while loving someone deeply gives you courage." - Lao Tzu

People tell me I have been so "strong" through all of this- Andie is the reason I am strong, because I can draw strength knowing he loved me to the depths of his soul. Because I loved him so deeply, I have courage to move forward knowing he is always with me and the girls.

He loved me with all that he had, and I him. In fact, we still do...

Thu Oct 7, 2010 | 08:17 AM |
Holding on to letting go...

"There is no pain so great as the memory of joy in present grief." - Aeschylus

I've been listening to my new Randy Rogers CD a lot lately and the song "Holding on to letting go" kind of speaks to me. The song doesn't so much pertain to my life but the title sure does.

I haven't "let go" of much because I don't want to move on without Andie. The stack of cards on my dresser just keeps getting bigger, the flags presented to me at his funeral are still in the same place I set them when I got home that day, his boots are still by his chair in the bedroom where he left them, and so on.

Yesterday I "let go"... but just a little. I needed to reorder checks from the bank and so I got online and hit "quick reorder". Up pops a picture of how my checks will look and the bank is asking me to verify that all the information is correct. There I stare, for what seemed like an eternity at "Andie or Brooke Simmons" on the top of the checks. I knew I needed to take his name off-he can't write checks now, after all. "No," I told myself, "you can do it later." I almost hit confirm, then I stopped... "Push" yourself, this is a small step....so I hit edit and deleted his name, letter-by-stinkin'-letter. And *then* the tears started...AT WORK!!! This was the first time I've broken down at work. I actually had to leave my office and go to my car. I had to remind myself to breathe-how is something so mundane like ordering checks so traumatic?!?!?

In that moment it all became so definitive, permanent, finite, *real*...I was literally "deleting" him from a part of my life. I can still remember going to the bank after we got married and combining our bank accounts. I was giddy with excitement that we were merging our lives- two became one. And now, I've come full circle.

So, I'm "holding on to letting go" and digging in my heels. No surprise there for those of you who know how stubborn I can be! The universe will have to pry him from the grips of my love and I won't let go until I'm damn good and ready (and even then, it will be little by little).

Mon Oct 11, 2010 | 05:35 PM |
Grief- the condensed version

The other night I awoke feeling unsettled, I don't remember waking from a dream or what exactly woke me up, but I was restless and felt like I needed to journal. Allie was in bed with me so I grabbed my journal and snuck to the bathroom where I could turn on the light and jotted down my thoughts. I went right back to bed, quickly fell back to sleep, and had totally forgotten about the incident until last night when I flipped back a few pages looking for another entry and saw it...it's a version of my grief story condensed in a metaphorical context- yes, I really just said metaphorical context, I'm a nerd. I am choosing to share this so others can understand grief without having to ask someone who is grieving all the nitty gritty details that you're really too afraid to ask anyway.

Losing Andie was like being caught in a rip tide- my feet were pulled out from under me and I went under- disoriented, not knowing which way was up. Instinctively I found the surface and burst through gasping for air and for a second you think it's all going to be okay, only to find yourself farther from shore- adrift at sea with no bearings or sense of direction. At first you want to fight the current but realize that to survive you must tread water and ride the waves hoping that someone will appear ready to help and throw you a life preserver.

Every now and then I still get the urge to fight the waves- I'm learning to ride them. I would not be surviving without my best friend Shannon, and most importantly my Mom. They are my saviors.

Here's honoring the "life preservers" in my life- my best friend, my brain's other half, my confidant Shannon- and my ridiculously supportive, always ready to lend a hand, self-sacrificing mother. I love y'all!

Mon Oct 11, 2010 | 06:20 PM |
My everything...

"If you lose hope, somehow you lose the vitality that keeps life moving, you lose that courage to be, that quality that helps you go on in spite of it all. And so today, I still have a dream."
- Martin Luther King, Jr.

My daughters: my inspiration, my hope, my courage, my dream.

Fri Oct 15, 2010 | 08:30 PM |
Friendship

"When we honestly ask ourselves which person in our lives means the most to us, we often find that it is those who, instead of giving much advice, solutions, or cures, have chosen rather to share our pain and touch our wounds with a gentle and tender hand. The friend who can be silent with us in a moment of despair or confusion, who can stay with us in an hour of grief and bereavement, who can tolerate not knowing, not curing, not healing and face with us the reality of our powerlessness, that is a friend who cares." - Henri Nouwen

Wow! Isn't that powerful and thought provoking- and SO true! It is hard to really just *BE* with someone who is in pain and not feel the need to talk through it or offer condolences. It has been interesting to see how people have reacted to me in my "time of mourning". The friends who I thought would be right there at my beck and call, now suddenly stand back in the shadows, rarely making contact, afraid to reach out (probably more so because of their own issues than mine) and the people who were periphery friends now step up to the plate and jump in full force ready to help. Often checking in when I least expect it.

I have no judgment of either group, for I have been on both sides of the grief journey more than once. I understand the lack of understanding and the not knowing what to do or say in certain situations. I understand what it's like to have questions but be afraid to ask or pry. I know how uncomfortable it is to be with someone and bear witness to their pain and not be able to help.

I've heard it said that people come into our lives to teach us lessons, and they leave when the lesson has been learned. I guess there is no better time to learn some lessons than now. I am saddened to think that some people will slowly disappear from my life because they knew me through Andie and now there is not that connection anymore, yet I understand that it is also the natural course of things. In a way I welcome the reprieve from some people whose relationship feels like an obligation or something that must be maintained, to make way for new friends who bring fulfillment to my life. On the other hand, I don't want to lose any connection to what my life with Andie used to be.

I wonder what lessons I've learned from those who will now fade from my life, and what lessons I've imparted to them. I'm excited to think about what new things I will learn from those making more of an appearance in my life. While I am afraid of my future for the first time in my life, I am also curious and hopeful about what it will bring.

Mon Oct 18, 2010 | 09:24 AM |
Life goes on...

"In three words I can sum up everything I've learned about life: it goes on" - Robert Frost

I was in a funk for most of the beginning of the weekend knowing that the 4-month anniversary was coming up. I had dinner plans with friends on Friday that got cancelled and Mom had to leave shortly after I got home from work on Friday, so there I sat with nothing to do and the thought of spending a weekend alone was crushing. I felt so abandoned and couldn't see past the moment of despair...these beautiful weathered weekends were supposed to be spent with my husband and children doing fun activities, not alone handling two busy toddlers all by myself for one more monotonous night of dinner/bath/bedtime routine. I was so lonely and alone and sad and angry and pitiful and pathetic. I could go on and on...basically I just couldn't *push* past those feelings so I didn't. I did what any self-respecting widow would do: I wallowed in them and let myself feel it all, and wouldn't ya know it- just like a toddler throwing a tantrum, once it was all out I was over it. Within minutes!

The good news is that my evening went on to get better and so did the weekend. Me and the girls had a fun evening spending time alone together. The very next day Addison took her first steps. It was such a joyful and exhilarating experience and I was so glad that I was home with her to see it happen. Of course it was bittersweet that Andie wasn't there in person but I could feel his presence. On Sunday I got together with my close girl friends at the lake for the afternoon and had a nice time. We usually get together on the 18th of the month to commemorate the anniversary of Andie's passing and help me through what is usually a rough day, but we did it a day early this month due to schedule conflicts. It was of course a beautiful day and I could almost visualize Andie standing on the dock at the lake house fishing. It was the kind of day he would have loved. The evening wrapped up with dinner at my house with Andie's side of the family. All of the sudden, I wasn't feeling so abandoned or alone- I was feeling loved and supported and embraced.

So life *does* go on despite the fact that I don't want it to, or that the *way* that it's going on is not really convenient for me, or what I had planned. Life goes on and your children walk for the first time, and you spend quality time with really good friends, you watch your children kiss their grandmother, and you continue to celebrate the little things you can find joy in.

Wed Oct 20, 2010 | 11:11 AM |
The price of healing...

"Money often costs too much." -Ralph Waldo Emerson

The other day while sitting at the lake and having a few minutes to myself I was reflecting on all the things Andie and I had dreamed about: buying a boat, having a lake house, building our dream home on our 2.5 acres, traveling, getting him a new truck, etc. They were all things we couldn't afford to do, or felt would be irresponsible to do when there were things like retirement and college funds that needed more immediate attention. We always thought we would "get to it" later....it occurred to me that the irony of my situation is that now, thanks to life insurance, I have the money to actually afford those things but I don't want them. I could go out and buy a boat, or a lake house, or both...but I don't want to because there is no joy in it without Andie to share it with.

So there it sits in an account earning interest (I am nothing if not responsible and practical, after all) becoming an ever larger, looming, burden...and I have *NO* desire to spend it. Whatever I bought with it would seem tainted to me, like I would always know in the back of my mind I traded Andie for this house, or boat, or whatever...

The joy of spending money comes from working hard to earn it. I didn't rightfully earn the money I now have- I *sacrificed* my most precious gift for it. I lost my husband, my life, my everything, and got several big checks in return...how messed up is that? I have apathy towards the money, a hatred for it, a denial that it even exists because it represents my husband's life and puts a value on something that is priceless. To put a numerical value on what a person is worth is impossible, and absurd. He deserves *so* much more, *I* deserve so much more, my *kids* deserve so much more. Not more money- more time, more hugs, more intimate moments, more laughs, more *life*! Whoever said money doesn't buy happiness was right on- I can't buy my way out of this pain. There is no price on healing.

So, yeah, the money I have *did* cost me too much...and it so wasn't worth it.

Thu Oct 21, 2010 | 01:03 PM |
You're gonna think I'm crazy...

Andie connected with me from the other side. I've been touched by an angel. There, I've said it. Out loud- to the whole world.

17

You probably think I'm crazy; I did too...until it happened for the third time last night.

Last night was a difficult night. The girls went down without a peep right on time so I decided to go take a bath and wind down myself. Suddenly Allie starts crying- I wait- she keeps crying. After about 5-10 minutes I decide I better get out of the tub and go deal with her before she wakes Addie up. This pattern has been going on with her for almost two weeks- she goes down right on time, falls quickly asleep, then wakes about 2 hours later crying or ready to play. I brought her to bed with me to try to calm her and she would not be still, constantly moving positions, crawling, bouncing, babbling, etc. After a while I put her back in bed and told her she was just going to have to cry it out because it was her bedtime, and now mommy's bedtime. I let her cry for 10 minutes then went back in to calm her. When I left she cried again, and I mean *screamed* for 20 full minutes- it was excruciating to watch the clock and pray she would just exhaust herself, and she *never* did. Then the dreaded happened- Addie woke up too, so now they were both crying. And I was fuming.

I tried holding and calming them in their room but to no avail, so into my bed all three of us piled. They nitpicked at each other, played with each other, stole each other's pacifiers, they did everything but go to sleep. After about 10-15 minutes I had had it, back to bed they both went. I decided I would steel myself and they could both cry themselves to sleep. Mother of the year? I was not. Patron saint of patience? Not even close.

Addie went down right away...Allie fought it, and fought it, and fought it...now we are looking at close to an hour of her refusing to sleep and screaming at the top of her lungs. I flung myself out of bed and stomped into her room. I picked her up to bring her back to bed with me and told her, "You are really frustrating me, and your daddy isn't helping me out any!" I figure if he had to die, the least he could do is help me out from the other side, right? Doesn't he have some special powers now that he's an angel, can't he see I'm having a hard time and somehow send calming vibes to the girls, or to *me*? Can't he give me *something*?!?!

I promise this is going somewhere, just bear with me...

So I lay Allie down on my pillow and I lie down next to her and nuzzle my face in her neck, inhaling the sweet baby smell, telling myself to calm down and take a deep breath. And for the first time, she lies perfectly still and gets quiet. She dozes off within mere minutes then shifts position and rolls over on my chest and throws her sweet little arm around my neck. As I start to doze off I get a sensation right behind my ear...I've had this sensation twice before and I'm convinced it's Andie making contact with me from the other side.

I can't even describe the feeling; it's like an energy on my skin. The sensation that something is touching me, but not touching me at the same time, sort of similar to the hair rising on the back of your neck but the hair isn't rising, there are no goose bumps and it's localized to one specific spot. It's like if you hold your hand millimeters away from your face and close your eyes, you can feel the presence of your hand, the energy from it, but you know that something is not actually touching you.

It startled me a bit because it started out faintly then got stronger, I actually reached my hand around and felt behind my ear to see if something like the sheet, or Allie's hand had wandered up there, and there was actually a perfectly good reason for the sensation. There wasn't anything there and the feeling continued a little longer then faded away. I am convinced that he heard my plea of needing help and he answered, he calmed Allie down in the few seconds it took me to walk from her bedroom to mine and lay her down. Then he touched me to let me know he was there supporting me.

It's happened two other times before. I really thought that I was just going crazy, or making things up in my head, but now that it's happened a third time I'm convinced that he is showing me

19

he is here. Every night before I fall asleep I talk to him and ask him to give me a sign he's here and to visit me in my dreams. The first time it happened I was lying in bed and in that state between awake and asleep where you don't have all your senses about you. I got the feeling that something was lying on top of me, there was a weight on me and I couldn't move. It woke me up fully, and I had the distinct sensation that Andie had just been lying with me. That was only a couple of weeks after he died and I wrote it off as part of my imagination and being in the crazy throes of grief. Even my mom kind of looked at me like I was going cuckoo when I told her about it.

The second time it happened was much like last night, I was lying in bed and this energy sensation appeared on my temple, almost like he was kissing me goodnight, or brushing my hair away from my face. Each time that it has happened the feeling has lingered long enough for me to become fully awake and aware of myself, so I know that it's not something I'm dreaming.

I choose to believe that he hears me, and knows when I need him, and is sending me a sign that our love and connection still endures.

Even if that makes me crazy...

Sat Oct 23, 2010 | 09:48 PM |

My "purple heart"

The Purple Heart is a United States military decoration awarded in the name of the President to those who have been wounded or killed while serving with the U.S. military.

It occurs to me that many of you may not know the exact story of what happened to Andie. In a nutshell, he had heart disease that led to a fatal arrhythmia while we were on vacation at my family reunion. One minute things were fine, the next minute they weren't. It was sudden, and unexpected, and traumatic.

It was like I entered a war zone. This is how I received my "purple heart" for being wounded in the line of duty as a wife.

While the emergency team worked on him in the ER they allowed me to sit beside him and hold his hand and talk to him. They even got me a stool and I remember being concerned that I would be in their way. I never let go of his hand, and never stopped telling him that I needed him to hang on. The doctor told me that they had gotten to a place where they needed to stop trying to save him, but that if I wanted them to they would keep working on him a little longer. Of course I asked that they continue, all the while knowing that even if they got him back he had been without oxygen long enough that there would be permanent damage, and he would not be the Andie that we all knew and loved. After another round of medications, and shocks, and CPR, and all efforts- there was still no heart beat. The doctor looked at me and our eyes locked, and I knew what the next moment would bring- I had to let him go.

It's funny the things you think about in moments of extreme stress. I looked at the clock and it was roughly a quarter to midnight, and I asked if they could wait and not call the time of death until after midnight because then it would be 6/19- I did not want him to die on 6/18 because that was his niece's birthday and I didn't want his death to overshadow her life. The doctor told me that it was too long to wait and they needed to go ahead and pronounce him. All I could say was, "okay". I stayed on that stool holding his hand, kissing it, and caressing it on my cheek for what seemed like an eternity.

The necklace I wear with Andie's wedding ring on it was put on me that night by a nurse and I haven't removed it since that moment. The trauma team had gone and a nurse came in to turn off the machines. I was in the room alone with him and the nurse, and she asked me if I wanted his necklace. I said I did, so she removed it from his body with such tenderness; almost like she was afraid to hurt him. She went to the sink to wash the vomit off of it and brought it back to me. She asked if I wanted to wear it, I said I did. In that moment of silence as she put the necklace on me and clasped it, my world shifted. The finality of all that had just happened hit me. The necklace that I had never seen my husband without was now around my neck. In that moment the nurse showed me the meaning of human connection- silence between us with a thousand words unsaid. I don't even know her name but she will always hold a very special place in my heart and in my memories for her loving act of compassion.

So I wear his necklace with his wedding ring on it like it is a war wound, my "purple heart", my "medal of valor". It's my symbol to the world of what I've been through. I feel almost as strongly about removing it as I do my wedding rings. I find myself toying with it during the day, slipping his wedding ring on my own finger, touching my hand to it when I speak of him. Often I don't even know that I'm doing it, it's like my subconscious way of reaching him.

That necklace is a symbol of our last moments of connection as husband and wife. Where he ended, I began.

Mon Oct 25, 2010 | 08:19 PM |
The color of a widow...

Black is the color of mourning but I've come to believe gray is the color of a widow. The widow's world is overshadowed by guilt, regret, doubt, uncertainty, and gloominess once the actual mourning has subsided and we begin to "move on" and establish a new normal. So to me, gray is the most appropriate shade.

Guilt and regret are the most salient emotions for me these days...there are a thousand decisions along the way that if I'd made differently might have resulted in a different outcome for Andie.

As I was walking with the girls the other day on the familiar route that Andie and I used to jog together, a memory ran through my mind like a jumpy movie reel- fleeting snippets passing through my consciousness. A few weeks before he died he had complained that he got short of breath when we were running. This was one such occasion, and he had to slow down and quit running. He told me to go on ahead without him and finish the run- he would walk home behind me. I remember turning to him and saying, "Oh yeah right, with my luck you'll have a heart attack and drop dead and there will be no one here to save you, and I'll just be waiting for you at home. I'm not leaving you." So we walked the rest of the way home together. The irony of that situation is that I didn't leave him, and when he did "drop dead" from heart problems I was lying right beside him in bed. I stayed by his side until he passed from this world, and despite the fact that I was right there with him I still couldn't save him. So it didn't matter after all, except that it gives me peace to know that he was not alone in those last moments and that I was there the whole time.

I have a lot of guilt over not being able to do more to save him- not acting quicker, wishing I hadn't gone into panic mode, not knowing what to do. I regret making the flippant comment that "with my luck" he would drop dead. I regret that I didn't make him go see a cardiologist after he couldn't finish our normal run. I regret that we went on vacation and were miles from the nearest hospital when he died. There is guilt that in an effort to lessen his anxiety about his chest pain, I tried to act as if it was just something minor instead of being honest with how scared I was. I regret that we chose to have his doctor look at him on Monday when we returned from vacation instead of going right in on Friday morning. There is guilt that perhaps I didn't tell him enough how much I loved him or how much he meant to me. There is guilt about all the fights and things said in the heat of the moment over the years that were hurtful. I regret that this past year of having twins was one of the most difficult years in our marriage and I didn't have more patience with him.

My guilt colors my world. There is a dense fog over my perceptions. It makes me second guess all the decisions I've made and will have to make. What if I do it wrong again, what consequences will I have to suffer the next time around?

Guilt: the feeling of a widow and regret it's close cousin...tandem shades of gray.

Thu Oct 28, 2010 | 08:22 AM |
Tracks of my tears

This morning on my way to work I decided to change out some of the CDs in my CD player. One I chose was a Motown/Golden Oldies mix that I put together years ago with artists like Smoky Robinson, The Supremes, Otis Redding, The 4 Tops, etc. Not sure why I chose that one, other than it must have been my unconscious trying to work some things out.

You see, we used to vacation in Kerrville every summer at our family's one room cabin with no a/c, no TV, no phone, etc. All we had was a radio that was always tuned to the oldies station- my dad loved oldies and especially when we were at the cabin. I think it reminded him of his own childhood summers spent there. Immediately when my CD came on I was taken back to when I was about 8 years old. The sound of oldies on the radio slipping through the screen door while me and my brother climbed trees, or played tag, or explored the woods around the cabin. This was the place where my father taught us to find arrowheads, and make flint rocks spark (in the unlikely event that we ever get lost in the woods and needed to build a fire), roasted marshmallows on the open fire pit, and hiked nature trails with us. It was like a time warp- we did all the things that he and his brothers did when they explored those same woods and hills when they were kids.

So this morning I was taken back to this place in my mind and I realized that in just over a month, my father will have been gone for 15 years. Half of my life. I was struck by the eerie similarities of losing him and losing Andie. They both died unexpectedly of heart conditions that were unknown to all of us at the time. They both were taken way too soon, leaving a wife and two children behind. They both could have been saved if medical intervention had gone the way it should have. And *then,* there's Kerrville-the place my father loved the most and I practically grew up, the place where Andie's parents grew up and graduated high school, the place we were vacationing when Andie died.

Now, as an adult, looking back through my not-so-rose-colored glasses, that place has lost its charm for me. There isn't a sense of nostalgia when I think of Kerrville-there is a sense of dread. It makes me think of the two most important men in my life, both of whom are gone and never to return.

I picture it like a black hole on a map- something to be avoided for fear of what could happen next. Like the Bermuda Triangle smack dab in the middle of Texas- there are warning signs, "Do Not Pass Through- Go Around!" It makes me abundantly sad to think that a place that used to hold so many happy memories is now something I want to avoid thinking about. I feel like the universe is trying to teach me a lesson, as if it is saying, "You didn't get it the first time around, do you get it *now*?" I'm still not sure I do...I'm continually trying to find meaning in all of this.

Now as I type this, I find myself humming a song that got stuck in my head this morning...

So take a good look at my face
You'll see my smile looks out of place
If you look closer, it's easy to trace the tracks of my tears
- Smoky Robinson & The Miracles

Sat Oct 30, 2010 | 08:49 PM |
Whisper of a touch

A man I barely know touched my shoulder in conversation recently and I bristled. My body actually stiffened on a noticeable level. I realized that this sort of innocent touch happens often between two who are intimate, such as husband and wife.

Like when I would be at the sink washing dishes and Andie would need to wash his hands- our bodies would brush against each other. Or when I was cooking dinner and he would lightly kiss the back of my neck as he walked by. Sometimes when we were both in a rush to get ready and would end up in the closet picking out clothes at the same time we would bump into each other. I remember our arms touching in the car as we both would rest an arm on the center console- often this would lead to us holding hands for a few seconds, or me rubbing his arm. I think of passing each other in a doorway, he was almost as broad as the doorway and we would both have to turn sideways to make it through but we would have a moment of connection. I remember touching his shoulder often when I talked to him, just like the man who recently touched mine. When I would hand him one of the babies while he was sitting on the couch and our legs would rub against each other. Or our fingers would meet for a second as I was handing him the car keys. The most comforting closeness was lying in bed next to each other and feeling the presence of him- often in the night he would roll over and lean against me.

It reminds me of the studies I've read about infants in Russian orphanages that are left in their cribs almost 24 hours a day with no cuddling and no touch. The psychological damage of that is lifelong and they often go on to develop numerous psychological problems, failure to thrive, or Reactive Attachment Disorder. To know that something so easy to give and so rewarding for both people involved is the very thing that keeps these babies from thriving is truly heartbreaking.

The catch phrase "Reach out and touch someone" holds significant meaning- we need touch, connection, and validation from another that we exist and are important and are valued. Funny how an innocent pat on the shoulder can hold so much meaning; "I'm still alive and noticed," it says. I'm usually one that has a definite "bubble"- I've never been a hugger. But these days I'll soak up any kind of touch I can get- I even welcome hugs and the requisite intrusion of my "bubble".

Of course I miss the kind of touch we all think about; hugs, kisses, holding hands, shoulder rubs.

But what I miss the most is the whisper of a touch...those barely perceptible moments of connection that you don't even realize you have.

Until they're gone...

Tue Nov 2, 2010 | 03:38 PM |
The business of dying...

There is a lot to be done after one dies, lots of loose ends to tie up, lots of people to call. The insurance company, the mortgage company, the banks, the lawyers, social security, pension companies, and on and on...it seems to never end.

On my way home from work the other day I was driving down Highway 46- the same route we came home from vacation after he died and a memory flashed through my mind.

The morning after he died my aunt was driving us home and the organ donation lady called. I never knew what went into organ donation or how involved it is. It was probably the most surreal and ridiculous conversation I've ever had, and even more so because my husband had only been dead for a few short hours. After discussing which parts of my husband's body they would likely "harvest"- an interesting choice of words, I thought, she had to ask me a litany of questions that seemed bizarre at the time. (Had he ever engaged in homosexual sex, slept with anyone from a certain region in Africa, or slept with anyone else who might have slept with someone from a certain region in Africa, had he ever used IV drugs, was he HIV positive, etc.) I remember when she asked me if he had ever engaged in homosexual sex I sarcastically retorted, "I think he'd rather be where he is right now than do that." Then the gravity of the situation hit me again and I realized I was talking about my dead husband- I felt guilty for making light of it. The topic of conversation was too heavy to handle at the moment...

I just received a draft version of my will and advanced directive in the mail from my estate attorney. I have to review it and make sure that I made all the right decisions about what goes where, and who gets my kids, and how my money will be handled if I die. We should have done this before Andie died but of course we thought we had more time. It's utterly depressing to think about your own mortality especially when the wound of grief is so fresh and you don't have the "*if* this should ever happen to us" buffer that most of us carry with us when we're young. I guess we never got around to doing it because the thought of tragedy was too heavy to handle at the time...

The hardest part is trying to decide what to put on his gravestone. I mean, how do you reduce a person to just a few words on a gravestone? I'm writing a letter to the girls about him and it is already 5 typed pages long. How do I condense all that into something meaningful and true and honest? I'm just not sure that anything I put on there will really do him justice, because he is after all, so much more than what a few words can convey.

It weighs heavy on my mind these days,
this business of dying...

Wed Nov 3, 2010 | 08:22 PM |

Taken...

I hate weather like this. Absolutely hate it. Always have.

Overcast, cold, blustery days leave me wanting a fire in the
fireplace and a cozy spot on the couch. Andie would always build
me a fire on nights like this, taking pride in making a huge
roaring fire. Men seem to like fire...I guess that goes back to the
caveman days and wanting to protect and provide for their
women. Andie definitely protected and provided for me in a
million ways, but tonight I think of him building a fire to keep
me warm, and standing back as the flames danced and flickered
to admire his work. He was always taking care of me in simple
ways- putting gas in my car, cleaning the kitchen, making coffee
in the morning, feeding the dogs, taking out the trash. Working
hard so we could have the things we dreamed about- the house,
the cars, the *life*. I glance at my wedding ring-to me it is the
ultimate symbol of his commitment to provide for me always.

These days I find myself looking at the hands of other people
while at the grocery store, the gas station, the car next to me.
Searching for wedding rings, and wondering...are they married?
What's their story? Are they spoken for? Do they have someone
to take care of them? Even if they have a ring on I wonder, are
they widowed like me and wearing it as a disguise? Are they
happily married, would they rather be divorced? Funny, I never
cared about the rest of the world and their marriage statuses
because mine was so perfect and it was all I needed. I was
spoken for and didn't concern myself with the status of others. I
have always been proud to wear my ring to show the world that I
belonged to someone- to prove to the world that I was worthy
and loved.

Oh, how blessed to be *provided* for,
spoken for,
taken...

Thu Nov 4, 2010 | 11:18 AM |
I will remember you...

This evening I will be attending a grief seminar at the church
and there will be a memorial ceremony in which a candle will be
lit for all those who've passed on over the last year.
I listened to this song by Sarah McLachlan on my way to work
today and thought it quite appropriate for what my evening
holds. (More on Sarah McLachlan to come in later posts, as she
has been inspiring me lately.) The interesting thing is that I used
to listen to this song and think of my dad after he died.

Now it holds a deeper, more profound meaning for me.

I will remember you
Will you remember me
Don't let your life pass you by
Weep not for the memories
I'm so tired but I can't sleep
Standin' on the edge of something much too deep
It's funny how we feel so much but we cannot say a word
We are screaming inside, but we can't be heard
But I will remember you
Will you remember me
Don't let your life pass you by
Weep not for the memories
I'm so afraid to love you, but more afraid to lose

Clinging to a past that doesn't let me choose
Once there was a darkness, deep and endless night
You gave me everything you had, oh you gave me light
And I will remember you
Will you remember me
Don't let your life pass you by
Weep not for the memories

I love you Dad. I love you Andie. And I *will* remember you.

{PART TWO}

SEARCHING...

Do not be conformed to this world, but be transformed by the renewal of your mind, that by testing you may discern what is the will of God, what is good and acceptable and perfect.
Romans 12:2 ESV

Sat Nov 6, 2010 | 12:28 PM |
Hold on...

Hold on
Hold on to yourself
For this is gonna hurt like hell
Hold on
Hold on to yourself
You know that only time will tell
What is it in me that refuses to believe
This isn't easier than the real thing
My love
You know that you're my best friend
You know I'd do anything for you
Let nothing come between us
My love for you is strong and true
Am I in heaven here or am I...
At the crossroads I am standing
Oh god if you're out there won't you hear me
I know that we've never talked before
Oh god the man I love is leaving
Won't you take him when he comes to your door
Am I in heaven here or am I in hell
At the crossroads I am standing
Hold on
Hold on to yourself
For this is gonna hurt like hell...
(Excerpt from "Hold On"- by Sarah McLachlan)

I hear often from others how strong I am, or how well I'm handling things...my take on it is a little different. The work of grief can only be done by the person grieving, for each person's grief is unique.

So I hold onto myself, I cling to myself, to push me through this. Though I do lean on others for support, really the only person that can truly get me through this is me. So maybe that's where the strength comes from. Knowing *I'm* the one that has to take each step forward, *I'm* the one who has to wake up each

33

morning and make a choice to get through each day, to *push myself onward.*

I don't think it is strength- it just is what it is…the experience of all who grieve. When you get down to the core of the issue you know it's *you* that has to make it through.

Not anybody else.

Nobody else can carry the burden of grief for you, nor should they.

You just have to "hold on"…

Sun Nov 7, 2010 | 08:31 AM |
Prayer rations…

Does God ration answered prayers?

Did he answer too many prayers for us in the couple of years before Andie died when we prayed every night that I would make it through the pregnancy, and that the girls and I would be healthy?

I'm the one with a congenital heart condition that made carrying a baby extremely dangerous, and when we found out I would be carrying two babies…we held our breath and prayed. Carrying multiples automatically makes you a high-risk pregnancy, but carrying multiples with a precarious heart condition-well, that's as risky as it gets. We took a calculated risk getting pregnant and breathed a sigh of relief when there were no adverse complications for the girls or me. When Andie's mom was diagnosed with cancer we prayed daily for her to be healed, for her life to be spared, and the cancer to go away. And it did.

We thought it was miraculous that all our prayers were answered in the 18 months before he died. Leaving me wondering now...was it not miraculous, but just God keeping score? Marking hash marks on some big chalkboard in the sky.

Did we use up all our prayers and that's why the last prayers I prayed while sitting in that ambulance, begging for him to stay alive, went unanswered? Did God not answer me because I used up my allotment and it was someone else's turn to get the good fortune?

It should have been me that died; I was the one that the odds were against...

Mon Nov 8, 2010 | 08:35 AM |
You just gotta have faith...

I knew my last post was going to create quite a stir and lots of conversation. "Strong" believers always have the clichéd things to say such as:

There is a reason you will know someday.
God has his purpose.
We are not to question our God, but just to believe in him.
Just have faith.
God will not give us more than we can handle.

I know some will call my faith weak because I question God, but I say "Who are we *not* to question God?" I believe that my God gave us free will and the ability to question and make our own decisions for a reason. If he wanted us to all blindly follow his ways he would not have given us free will. I believe in a God that is so confident and steadfast that he knows that even when our faith is tested and we doubt him that we will see the light and come around with a renewed strength of faith.

Those with a "blind" faith who never question are just accepting what they have been told. Those who seek enlightenment and knowledge on their own and *still* have faith in God despite their

35

unanswered questions, have a conviction that is born out of pain, tragedy, struggle, and triumph. It is a faith that is won in a hard fought battle, but won nonetheless. It is a faith that is *earned*, not bestowed upon them by acceptance of a religious doctrine.

I believe that relationships are strengthened through trials and tribulations, and when you both come out on the other side still able to say, "I'm here, I want to stay here, and I still love you," then you have reached a new level of commitment- for me it is the same with God. I believe in a God that wants us to question, that allows us to be angry with him, that understands the need to test his limits, because he ultimately welcomes the opportunity to continue to prove to us that he is here and working in our lives.

So is there a reason that Andie had to die? I'm still not sure I can swallow this one; it's hard to believe that there would ever be a good enough reason for my children to not know their father. But maybe the reason is to renew my faith in Him and strengthen it. Maybe everyone else is right, and I'll know the reason one day.

My faith is stronger because I have been to the brink of wanting to forsake my God, yet I don't. He has given me every reason *not* to believe, yet I still do because the alternative is more than I can bear.

I *want* believe...I *have* to believe.

I just gotta have faith...

Tue Nov 9, 2010 | 07:53 PM |
Baggage claim...

Every so often I get the "someday you'll move on" speech from someone- happened just the other day in the doctor's office.

Someone who means well and has their heart in the right place, yet still feels it necessary to remind me that I am *indeed* a "young" widow, and *surely* I will find love again.

The truth is that most days I cannot fathom this, though the rational side of my brain knows it must be true because the intense loneliness and loss of companionship is awful, and I loved being married and having a companion. I loved nurturing someone and in return being idolized by them. It gives me hope to think that one day I can find love again.

I read in one of my grief books that people who had good, strong, happy marriages tend to move on into new relationships sooner than those who had difficult or unhappy marriages. The logic being that those who were unhappy have more reticence to get into another marriage because they have a bad taste in their mouth about the institution of marriage, and they tend to carry guilt about the poor state of the relationship which makes closure harder to attain. Those who were happy though, want that kind of connection again and see marriage as a valuable asset to their well being.

I certainly fall in the latter category and do want to find love again sometime in the future, but right now that seems like a *very* distant future, and frankly a betrayal of my love and commitment to Andie. And though I said til death do us part, and death *actually* did part us...it still doesn't feel like it yet (yes, there is still some denial going on here). I've joked to my closest friends that I did it for love the first time around, but the next time I'm gonna marry for money because the odds of me finding the perfect love like I had with Andie again is a million to one, so I better not hope for that. Truthfully, I don't think I'll ever get married again. I'm not opposed to dating or having a companion, but marriage is so sacred. I do believe that I found my true soul mate in Andie, and that I could never find another who fits me so perfectly. I think if I were to marry again I would always feel like I just settled for the next best thing. And I don't settle.

So I was thinking about what it would actually be like for some man to unwittingly walk into my life right now...boy would he be in for it! I wrote up my personal ad for when I think I'm ready to venture into the world of dating again...so here goes.

"Single, white, widow with twins seeking a self-sacrificing man that can understand he will *always* live in my dead husband's shadow, and he will never *really* be able to measure up. Must be willing to endure crying jags and temper tantrums on a moment's notice- either from me or one of my children. Willingness to take on mortgage payments and a part-time live in mother-in-law a plus! Seeking a man that will be okay with rarely having my undivided attention and who loves to help out around the house. Must want a perfectionistic and demanding woman, nicely packaged with a few signs of wear and tear (i.e. stretch marks and hail damage on the thighs). To claim your baggage call anytime- but leave a message as I probably won't be available to answer during working hours on a weekday, or between the evening hours of 5-9 as I'm busy with the dinner, bath, bed-time, clean the house, routine with twins."

And I think to myself,
Yeah, Good luck with that...

Thu Nov 11, 2010 | 10:15 AM |
Do what you have to do

I know you're all probably sick of my musical inspirations, but Sarah McLachlan is *really* speaking to me these days. It seems like every song on her Mirrorball CD has some significance for me. Again, my focus is on just doing what I have to do to get through the day. Yesterday was particularly hard- I felt distracted and on edge all day, short and irritable with those around me through no fault of their own.

I want to be with Andie so badly, to talk to him, to hug him, to smell him. I know there is no way to be with him until I meet

38

him again in heaven and that holds a special allure these days. Now don't get me wrong, I'm not suicidal- I just know that is the only way I can see him, so on bad days I find myself wishing my life would just hurry up and I could flash forward 50 years and pass quietly in my sleep and into his arms. The rest of the time I just do what I have to do...

Excerpts from "Do What You Have To Do" - by Sarah McLachlan

And fate has led you through it
You do what you have to do...
And I have the sense to recognize that
I don't know how to let you go
Every moment marked
With apparitions of your soul
I'm ever swiftly moving
Trying to escape this desire
The yearning to be near you
I do what I have to do
But I have the sense to recognize
That I don't know how
To let you go
A glowing ember
Burning hot
Burning slow
Deep within I'm shaken by the violence
Of existing for only you
I know I can't be with you
I do what I have to do
I know I can't be with you
I do what I have to do
And I have the sense to recognize, but
I don't know how to let you go

Yeah, what she said...

Sat Nov 13, 2010 | 09:45 PM |
Unsettled...

I've always had a plan, a 5-year plan, a goal, something to reach for in the future. It was all lined up, and now I don't have that. It's the first time in my life I feel uncertain and chaotic and exhilarated by the options. I have so many options and things I hadn't even thought about doing before Andie died. I feel unsettled in my life, like something needs to change...

Lately I've been thinking about my career a lot. A friend let me know about a possible job opening in another district next fall that would be a substantial pay increase, I've considered going back to school and becoming a Physician's Assistant, or getting my Ph.D. in psychology, or just focusing on my neuropsychology certification and doing more specialized contract testing. I've thought about picking up my life and moving to Costa Rica for a year to do something adventurous and to teach my daughters a second language. I've thought about selling my home and building the dream home that Andie and I had planned on our 2.5 acres in the hill country. I've also thought about selling the land in the hill country altogether...

I'm scared of all this because I've never been on such an uncharted path with no direction. I don't know how to do that, or *if* I should do that. It feels like anything I would reach, any goal attained would seem unfair because had he not died I would never have done those things. It's like this whole new life in front of me, no matter which path I choose is the wrong one because it's not the way it should've been or would've been.

Is it fair to go down a new path, and am I okay with that? Would I be able to accept it, or would I always feel guilty for moving on without him? I don't know. Maybe I stay in this life as penance and don't change a thing, and don't take a chance, and don't *push* myself to grow. Why do I feel the need to punish myself? What did I do wrong, why do I keep bearing the burden and taking on the responsibility for his death?

Survivor's guilt- that's a whole other topic for another day. Nah, on second thought...

I gotta push!

Tue Nov 16, 2010 | 11:47 AM |

The timepiece...

I have felt rather disengaged and uninspired with my psyche the past few days- hence the reason for no profound posting here today.

What I would like to let you all know about is an awesome shop I found on etsy.com that has incredibly unique jewelry and other fun trinkets from vintage items.

The timepiece Christmas ornaments are what intrigued me. They're old pocket watches made into Christmas ornaments. I commissioned a custom one in which the time reads 10:04.

As most of you know, October 4th was our wedding anniversary and we picked that date because Andie was a police officer. Being that he used the radio code "10-4" every time he responded on the radio, as in, "10-4, I'll be in route to the scene" or something like that... we figured he would never forget our anniversary that way. What most of you *might* not know is that I'm cheesy. And every time I would randomly look at the clock and see it was 10:04 I would point this out to him with excitement, and he would smile. Or roll his eyes. Or both. I always thought it was neat to catch this time on the clock, and often I would make him kiss me in honor of our marriage- no matter where we were when this happened. He *really* rolled his eyes if this happened in public as he was not one for PDA.

The cool thing is that lately I catch 10:04 on the clock a lot. A *whole* lot. At work, in the car, turning out the light and going to bed, while on the computer checking e-mail, when picking up my phone to make a call, etc. etc. A while back I had done my fastest run time ever and beat my personal record. When I checked the clock to see how long it took me-you guessed it, I finished the run at exactly 10:04 am! I just knew his spirit was running with me and pushing me.

Anyway, it happens *way* more than chance these days and I choose to believe this is a sign from him. Whenever it happens I send a little loving thought to him and I believe that this is our way of keeping up that mundane daily communication that I desperately miss.

So for my very first Christmas without him I decided that this very neat ornament with such a "special" time on it would be a good way to honor him.

Tue Nov 16, 2010 | 08:53 PM |
The necklace...

Tonight Addie did not want to go to bed. So I cuddled her on the couch. Just me and her in the quiet and stillness of the evening.

At first she was very calm and laid on my shoulder as if she was about to fall asleep. Abruptly she lifts her head with purpose, looks at me, then begins playing with my necklace. Only, it's his necklace really. With his wedding ring on it.

I tell her to lie down and try to guide her head to my shoulder. She resists strongly and continues to play with my necklace intently. After a few more failed attempts to get her to lie down, I turn her on her side and cradle her where she can still see the necklace- which she continues to play with. Then she starts putting his wedding ring up to my mouth. She continues pushing it on my lips until I kiss his ring. Then she wants me to do this several more times. If I don't kiss it, she just smashes his ring harder into my lips until I give in and kiss it. She's insistent about it.

As all of this is unfolding I'm wondering what made her do this. Is she thinking about him? Is he here with us in the room and she is picking up on his vibes? Is it possible that she *even* remembers him? He has been gone for 1/3 of her short life...can she *really* remember him?

Surely she is not smart enough to understand that the necklace I wear is his, and that the ring is his too. But, there *is* an innocent intuition about her. Right after he died I noticed that she and Allie both would look up to the sky, or get fixated on a point just beyond my gaze and hold it. It was almost eerie- like they could see him or sense him. And I can't help but think that maybe on some gut level she *does* understand the importance of this necklace. That she knows this necklace was my last connection to him, and his last moments with me.

Interestingly, all week I've contemplated taking the necklace off, watching for a sign to guide me in the right direction. Now, I feel like we are all connected to it more deeply than I realized. I feel it to my core.

This necklace and ring- symbolic of no ending and no beginning. Just a
solid,
never,
ending,
connection...

Thu Nov 18, 2010 | 03:43 PM |
The show must go on...

Andie's been gone 5 months today and I've settled into a new normal. A routine that is my "new" life as a single parent. A new way of doing things on my own. A one-man show. It is something I despise. It is a routine that is born out of necessity, not out of want. My everyday doing is empty and lonely and boring and mundane.

43

Get out of bed in the morning. No one to talk to while I get ready for work. No one to tell me I look pretty today.

Drive to work. No one to text when I get bored. No one to text me to say they are just thinking of me.

Drive home. No one to call to say I am on my way as was our ritual.

I come home and decide what the girls should eat for dinner with little regard for nourishing myself. I don't want to prepare a meal for one.

I bathe the girls and brush their teeth. No one to help me get them out of the tub.

I get them ready for bed and give them their nighttime cuddles- having to take turns with who gets to sit on my lap and who just gets to sit beside me. There isn't another lap for them to cuddle on.

I tuck them in and wish them sweet dreams- one child at a time. They must take turns with me as I only have one set of arms to carry them to bed.

I close up the house, check that the doors are locked, and turn out all the lights. No one to protect me in the quiet darkness.

I wash my face and brush my teeth- staring in the mirror at a reflection of a girl I don't know anymore. A girl I do not want to know.

I crawl into bed, thankful for the reprieve that sleep brings. No one to wish good night.

Then I do it all again the next day because, after all
the show must go on...

Mon Nov 22, 2010 | 09:00 AM |
Surrender...

Stubborn
Driven
Strong-willed
Determined
Perfectionist
Over-achiever
Independent

Yep, that's me. I'm the one who expects a lot from others but *always* expects more from myself. I push those around me to achieve but always push myself harder. It used to drive Andie crazy that I pushed him- I just always saw so much more potential in him than he saw in himself and wanted the best for him.

The other day my mom and I got into a little tiff because she had offered her opinion on something regarding the girls and I took it as her trying to tell me how to parent. In discussing this she says, "Brooke, as your mother it's hard for me because I think you always want to do things the hard way. I just don't want you to make things harder on yourself than it has to be,"...or something to that effect.

It struck me in that moment as so true. Most other times I would have argued with her, but this time it resounded deep within me. Why do I hold myself to a standard that I would never hold others too? Why do I always have to do things "by myself" or "my way"? I don't know the answers, but what I do know is that it is something I have to work on. Just because I've always been this way doesn't mean I have to continue to be this way. I'm a different person now than I was 5 months ago and though I hate it, I'm learning to accept it. Perhaps this is one more aspect of me that needs to change.

As my near constant source of inspiration these days, Sarah (McLachlan) says, "the life I've left behind me is a cold room".

Maybe I need to quit fighting it. Maybe it's time to surrender to all this.

This grief.
This process.
This rebirth of me...

Excerpts from "Sweet Surrender" - by Sarah McLachlan

It doesn't mean much
it doesn't mean anything at all
The life I've left behind me
Is a cold room
I've crossed the last line
From where I can't return
Where every step I took in faith
Betrayed me
And led me from my home
And sweet
Sweet surrender
Is all that I have to give
I miss the little things
I miss the simple things
Oh I miss everything
About you
So it doesn't mean much
It doesn't mean anything at all
The life I left behind m
Is a cold room

So today, this fighter is throwing in the towel.
I'm waving my white flag.
I surrender.

The "old" me? Doesn't mean much...

Wed Nov 24, 2010 | 06:58 PM |
Blah!

Ugh... I was *going to* surrender. I had every intention of giving it a valiant effort. The problem is... I can't. I'm a fighter. I don't give up and I don't give in.

I can't give in to this grief thing yet. I want to, or at least I *think* I do. I know I need to. But for some reason I just can't. I am stubbornly *NOT* accepting that this really is it. This sleep-deprivation, doing-it-all-alone, never-having-a-break life is what I'm stuck with.

To make a long story short, the girls have been extremely fussy, obstinate, and not sleeping through the night for the past 5 days- which makes for a mommy that is extremely fussy, obstinate, and not sleeping through the night. Not a good combo.

It is so draining to not have the other half of my tag team. There is no hope of passing the buck when he gets home from work in a few hours, or when he gets home from the ranch in a day or two...this is just a never ending reality with no end in sight and no reprieve to look forward to- I will do this alone for the rest of my life. At times it feels so hopeless.

I know I should be blogging about all the things for which I am grateful, instead of complaining about my lot in life. The truth is it all seems so cliché- of course I'm grateful for my children, family, friends, great support system, awesome job, blah, blah, blah.

What I'm not grateful for is like the elephant in the room. The big looming issue glaring me in the face. I'm not thankful, in fact, I'm quite bitter about so much. I think what hurts the most these days is that it didn't have to be this way. If medical intervention had proceeded as it *should* have when we sought it, then he would be sitting here with me. He'd be lamenting the crazy holiday schedule coming up, wondering what demons

47

have possessed our children in the past five days and looking up how to perform exorcisms on the internet, and happily refilling my wine glass. From a box, no less.

Yep, it's gotten that bad. I'm actually drinking wine from a box.

Sigh. Is it too early in the season to say, "Bah humbug"?

Fri Nov 26, 2010 | 01:24 PM |
Better late than never...

So it finally hit me today what I am thankful for this season. I know I'm literally a day late, and probably a dollar short and won't do this post justice to adequately express what's truly in my heart, but here goes...

I am thankful for all of *you*. All of my readers, all of my friends and family, all of you who support me in this widow walk. I've realized that the reason I blog and share some of my most private thoughts and moments of pain is because I continue to gain strength and comfort from all of you. Your feedback and comments and words of encouragement are what keep me going.

I know there are a lot of people who continue to pray for me and the girls, and who continue to send loving thoughts our way- for that I am eternally grateful. Without the cocoon of love and support I have, I would not be functioning. It is such a compliment, and little burst of joy in my day when I hear from one of you that I've inspired you, or given you hope, or that you understand me, or that you hurt for me. You all help me feel less alone, something I am deeply appreciative of. There are many of you who have kept me afloat for the day with your kind words.

I mentioned to someone the other day that I wanted some good to come out of Andie's death. I don't want it all to be for not. I find that maybe the good that can come is that I inspire you, give you hope, help you get perspective on your own life, as you all do for me- and hopefully there is a ripple effect. A pay it forward moment when you can do the same for someone else. And hopefully the cycle of giving continues- we are all able to give back to each other and lift each other up, making for a better world- even if it's just in a small way.

Cheers to all of you! Thank you seems so inadequate but I don't know what else to say. So,
Thank you!
Thank you!
Thank you!

Sun Nov 28, 2010 | 01:17 PM |
A picture is worth a thousand words...

When we were first dating one of the nicest gifts Andie got me was a really nice camera- the Canon Rebel (before they had the digital version). I loved that camera and did some of my best work on it. I thought I lost it once when I accidentally packed it when we were moving. After months passed and we couldn't find it he went out and bought me another one for my birthday. He knew how much that camera meant to me and how heartbroken I was to not have it. Ironically, we unpacked and found the old camera about a week after he bought the new one!

Andie was always proud of my photography. It was just a hobby I enjoyed, but he encouraged me to display some of my work in our home and always wanted me to try to sell my photos. I never thought I was good enough but he always did. When we'd see photography for sale for hundreds of dollars he'd always say, "You could do that. Your stuff is way better than this." His encouragement and admiration of me is one of the things I treasure and miss the most.

When they came out with the digital version of my Canon Rebel I *drooled* over it. *Pined* for it. *Longed* for it. But I never thought we could afford it, or should afford it, rather. I was always the one holding the purse strings saying we should put more into retirement or savings- not spend it on extravagant things we didn't really need. He wanted me to have the big expensive camera and tried to convince me to get it for years, but I always put it off because it was so expensive.

The weekend Andie died was Father's Day weekend. I had bought him a new lightweight digital camera as a gift. We had both been wanting a new camera for a while that was small enough to throw in my purse, so I splurged. I planned to give it to him Friday night when we arrived at our vacation destination so he could use it all weekend. Thursday afternoon he ran errands and came home with my "late" Mother's Day present; you guessed it- a new camera! We laughed and couldn't believe we both bought each other cameras. He felt bad that he never got me a Mother's Day present and said he wanted me to have it for our vacation.

When he bought this new camera he told me he had considered getting me the digital version of my really good camera. The Canon Rebel EOS...the only problem was the digital version starts at around $600 and goes up from there. He said he was sure I would be upset if he spent that much money, but that he would go back and get it if I *really* wanted it. Well, being practical I told him we shouldn't spend that much money on a camera and I would keep the small lightweight one he bought.

So we kept the practical camera. The one we could both use. Point and shoot- *so* easy. The problem is...I hate this camera. I thought I would like it because it's very compact and lightweight but it takes way too long between when you press the button and when the picture takes. My kids move so quick that I can never get a good shot. Something that would *never* happen with my Canon Rebel. I'm sure my vehemence towards this camera is only magnified by the fact that he gave it to me a day before he died- it's got bad juju in my mind.

He was often trying to buy me nice gifts, but hesitant because he knew I'd be mad about how much they cost. I should've let him buy me nice gifts more often. I'd have those things to treasure now. Another thing to add to my list of regrets...

So today I bought myself the digital Canon Rebel.

In honor of him.
In honor of his admiration for my photography skills.
In honor of the fact that it's only money- we can't take it with us when we die.

I bought the camera because he wanted me to have it. Because I wanted to have it.

Because photos are the only lasting thing we have after someone is gone, the only thing that can preserve a moment after our own memory fades, the only accurate historical representation of a life. I want to capture the moments that matter with my children- I don't want to be cursing the camera because it didn't shoot quick enough and the moment passed.

My children are changing so fast these days and I feel like I can't keep up. I want to always remember these moments of joy, laughter, and love with them.

I want to capture these moments and hold them close and never let them go...

Tue Nov 30, 2010 | 08:27 AM |
Ahem, ahem...here comes the soapbox

I'm in my angry phase again. I feel like there is no good or valid reason that Andie had to die. It could have been prevented a thousand ways.

Allow me to step onto my soapbox for a moment. Heart disease is one of the number one causes of death in America; it is largely because of our terrible diets and lack of exercise. After talking with the coroner about his death I learned that what killed him was a combination of genetic factors (predisposition for high cholesterol and heart disease) combined with a poor diet and lifestyle factors that only contributed to more high cholesterol and heart disease. His official cause of death was not even a heart attack. It was severe blockage of his coronary arteries (a condition called atherosclerosis) that led to his heart not being able to get blood and oxygen as needed. Basically, the coronary artery became blocked over time due to cholesterol and eventually it closed up completely- and he died. At only 34! Because he ate like crap for most of his life!

My concern is that people don't take their health, diets, and exercise seriously enough. Especially when we're young and think stuff like this only happens to older people. It only takes small changes to make a big impact. One small change we can all make is to eat less sugar-refined sugar, fructose, high fructose corn syrup, all forms of it!

Here is something I found while looking into this issue. It's a simple list put together about the dangers of sugar. I've put asterisks by the conditions that Andie had; all things that contributed to his death according to the coroner. He ate a diet high in processed foods and sugar until he started dieting about 10 months before he died. I believe with all my heart that if he had made lifestyle changes a lot earlier it would've been a different outcome.

Sugar can suppress the immune system.
Sugar can upset the body's mineral balance.
Sugar can contribute to hyperactivity, anxiety, depression, concentration difficulties, and crankiness in children.
***Sugar can produce a significant rise in triglycerides.
Sugar can cause drowsiness and decreased activity in children.
***Sugar can reduce helpful high density cholesterol (HDLs).

***Sugar can promote an elevation of harmful cholesterol (LDLs).

Sugar can cause hypoglycemia.

Sugar contributes to a weakened defense against bacterial infection.

Sugar can cause kidney damage.

***Sugar can increase the risk of coronary heart disease.

Sugar may lead to chromium deficiency.

Sugar can cause copper deficiency.

Sugar interferes with absorption of calcium and magnesium.

Sugar can increase fasting levels of blood glucose.

Sugar can promote tooth decay.

***Sugar can produce an acidic stomach.

Sugar can raise adrenaline levels in children.

Sugar can lead to periodontal disease.

Sugar can speed the aging process, causing wrinkles and grey hair.

Sugar leads to decreased glucose tolerance.

***Sugar can cause cardiovascular disease.

Sugar can contribute to diabetes.

Sugar can contribute to osteoporosis.

Sugar can cause a decrease in insulin sensitivity.

***Sugar can increase total cholesterol.

***Sugar can contribute to weight gain and obesity.

High intake of sugar increases the risk of Crohn's disease and ulcerative colitis.

***Sugar can increase systolic blood pressure.

Sugar causes food allergies.

Sugar can cause free radical formation in the bloodstream.

Sugar can cause toxemia during pregnancy.

Sugar can contribute to eczema in children.

Sugar can over stress the pancreas, causing damage.

***Sugar can cause atherosclerosis.

Sugar can compromise the lining of the capillaries.

Sugar can cause liver cells to divide, increasing the size of the liver.

***Sugar can increase the amount of fat in the liver.

Sugar can increase kidney size and produce pathological changes in the kidney.

Sugar can cause depression.
Sugar can increase the body's fluid retention.
Sugar can cause hormonal imbalance.
***Sugar can cause hypertension.
Sugar can cause headaches, including migraines.
Sugar can cause an increase in delta, alpha and theta brain
waves, which can alter the mind's ability to think clearly.
Sugar can increase blood platelet adhesiveness which increases
risk of blood clots and strokes.
Sugar can increase insulin responses in those consuming high-
sugar diets compared to low sugar diets.
Sugar increases bacterial fermentation in the colon.

If this doesn't scare you, I don't know what will. Decreasing the
amount of sugar we take in is a very small step towards bettering
our health. People look at me like I'm crazy around here when I
say I don't drink sweet tea. In Texas that's almost like saying you
don't believe in God. And I also don't allow my children to drink
it- *yes*, there are parents who start their kids on sweet tea in
Texas when they are still drinking out of sippy cups! I find it
appalling. It is my job as a parent to make responsible, healthy
food choices for my children while I still can. They will have all
their adult lives to make unhealthy decisions on their own.

So when I don't want my kids having tea, soda, or ice cream, or
any number of other treats...don't look at me like I'm a bad mom
who deprives her children of life's simple pleasures.
Acknowledge the good choice I'm making for them while they're
young- they don't know the difference now anyway. I'm not
opposed to an occasional treat-I promise, I *do* let them eat cake
on their birthday!

They already have risk factors genetically speaking, given what
happened to their father. I can't control that, but what I *can*
control is what they put in their sweet little mouths! And what I
put in mine for that matter. It's a struggle to make all the right
food choices, but I'm doing my best to be a responsible parent.

So I'm starting my new year's resolution now- less sugar for us all in the Simmons house! Think about your own diet and lifestyle and consider a small change you could make for the better- *Push* yourself to do it! Consider it a gift to those you love to better your own health.

We often say we'd die for the ones we love, instead why don't we choose to *really* live for them...

(Stepping down from the soapbox now)

Tue Nov 30, 2010 | 08:35 PM |
Numb...

I've been so numb and devoid of feeling lately. I walk around in an emotional haze- not really feeling the full effects of what has happened to me. I don't want to feel it. I don't want to accept it. I'm in a constant state of disbelief. Empty.

Tonight that all came crashing down. A neighbor dropped by and asked if I had any Christmas lights that needed to be hung. He was more than willing to do it for me if I needed- It was really no big deal, he explained. I knew it was a genuine, caring offer and the sweetness of this gesture sent me into a tailspin. It's a pain to hang lights; the very reason we never had them was because Andie refused to do it.

After the neighbor left it hit me: it's *so* real to everyone else that I don't have a husband.

It's just not real to *me*.
The rest of the world has accepted my fate.
I have not.

I can't make it seem real to myself except in small doses when I'm reminded like this, and when it does hit me it is overpowering. The pain is so deep that there aren't words to describe it. I guess this is why it's so hard to accept offers of help. Honestly, the offers wouldn't be there if I wasn't a widow. So, the second that I accept the offer it forces me to acknowledge what that person already knows- My husband is gone and he's not coming back. *Ever.*

Moments like this awaken me from my emotional catatonia. It jars my pain from the slumber it has been in. The Pandora's Box of feelings that I keep so tightly locked is opened, and the emotions come pouring out in full force. The protective cocoon I've woven that doesn't let the strong emotions in is cracked, and the real despair seeps in and invades my soul.

And ever so gently it seeps back out and I go numb again...

Thu Dec 2, 2010 | 09:59 AM |

Sustenance to last forever...

The other day (11/29/10) was the 15th anniversary of my father's death. I turned 30 this year, making it exactly half my life that he's been gone. Now that a few days have passed I realize that I'm on the downhill slide of it. Each new day that passes makes it longer that I have been without my father than I had with him.

I think about this with Andie, how in 10 years I will have been without him for as long as I had with him. And each new day after that will be longer without him than I had with him. The only saving grace in this is that what time I did have was beautiful, and meaningful, and awesome. What he gave me was fulfilling, and sustaining, and love at its finest. His love was sustenance for my soul.

And I wonder, can all the greatness that we had in a decade sustain me for the next 4 or so decades that I will have to live without him?

All I can do is hope...

Sat Dec 4, 2010 | 09:07 AM |
If I could...

If I could there is so much I would do, and change, and fix for my daughters. Their world has unfairly been turned upside down and what life they would've known is no longer an option. I often wonder about how this is going to irrevocably change who they are. Certainly growing up and having a good, strong, father figure would've had a profoundly different outcome for them than growing up without ever even remembering their father. Every time I see their angelic faces and think of their innocence lost through all of this I am deeply saddened. I dread the day they start asking questions and I have no good explanations.

As a parent my job is to protect them, provide for them, afford them all the best opportunities I can, and sometimes I feel powerless in all of this. I can't protect them from the pain of loss. I can't provide the experiences they would've had if they had two parents. I can't afford them all the same opportunities they are entitled to, as I am now a single parent. I am reminded of a song written by my uncle, Paul Hill.

"If I Could" by Paul Hill

If I could
I would write a song for you
A very special song for you
A song to lift you up when all your dreams have left you empty handed
If I could
I would be a friend to you
A very special friend to you
A friend that you could call whenever you just need someone to talk to
And if I could
I would stop the pain from ever getting through
I would keep this world from ever hurting you
If I could

I would give a smile to you
Yes, I would give a smile to you
A smile for anytime that things are not what they're supposed
to be
I know you've given more than one to me

At least once every few days, for just a millisecond, the thought passes through my head, "Andie is going to be so surprised to see how much they've changed when he gets home." It's like I think he's just been on a really long trip and will walk in the door any minute. My heart breaks for him and for the girls every time I am reminded that they have lost each other. Because the bottom line is, he lost out too. He was cheated in all of this too.

My daughters are my joy, my hope, my inspiration, my amusement, my whole life. They give so much more to me than I could ever give to them.

Oh girls, how things would be different for you if only, I could...

Sun Dec 5, 2010 | 08:18 AM |
Memory lane...

Yesterday I took a trip down memory lane...literally.

Andie's best friend, Eric, just had a new baby. So I went to see the family yesterday evening and took them dinner. The only problem is that they live on a street off of Lime Kiln Rd.

Lime Kiln Rd. is my own personal memory lane. Lime Kiln Rd. is the street that Andie and Eric lived on when I first met Andie. They rented this tiny little house out in the sticks, way down this winding country road called Lime Kiln Rd. You had to cross a cattle guard and drive down a dirt drive to get to the house. Last night I drove that road again for only the second time since Andie's been gone. (The first time I drove it I was still in such shock that none of the emotional association registered at the time.) I've driven that road a thousand times but last night was perceptibly different. Each twist and turn bringing back vivid memories.

That house on Lime Kiln Rd. is where I first met Andie, initially decided I didn't like him much, and then subsequently fell completely in love with him. It's where he would pursue me for almost two years before I would finally give him a chance.
That house on Lime Kiln Rd. is where he became my best friend. Where we would sit on the tailgate of his truck late into the night talking, and watching shooting stars across the Texas sky. That house on Lime Kiln Rd. is where I met his brother Roger for the first time, and he cornered me in the kitchen and implored me to *please* give his brother a chance because he knew Andie would treat me right and love me forever.

That house on Lime Kiln Rd. was home to many frat parties and bonfires and me being jealous that Andie was flirting with sorority girls and not me. That house on Lime Kiln Rd. is where I would watch movies with Andie in the dead of winter when they didn't have heat. I hate the cold more than anything, but I wanted to be near him so badly that I would wear my coat and cover up with a sleeping bag, eventually falling asleep with my head on his shoulder.

That house on Lime Kiln Rd. is where he would rub my back until I fell asleep. He wouldn't stop until I was asleep, and sometimes I would pretend that I was already asleep just so he would stop and get some sleep himself.

That house on Lime Kiln Rd. is where I went when I was falling apart during the lawsuit over my father's death. He took me to his room away from everyone, shut the door, and just held me while I cried.

It's where I hoped and prayed that he would kiss me for the first time, proving to me what everyone already said- that he was, in fact, in love with me. Lime Kiln Rd. is where we started. Where we fell in love. Where we reminisced about when we thought of the "good ol' days".

Lime Kiln Rd. is where my journey to him began.
It's my own personal memory lane.
And it's just not the same anymore.

Mon Dec 6, 2010 | 09:10 PM |

Equations...

The other day I was talking with a friend who is going through a rough time in her marriage. She was saying that she felt like there were only a few good months in all the years she's been married and the rest were wrought with turmoil. Now, I'm sure she is exaggerating a bit since the negatives always seem to outshine the positives when we are upset about something.

But, being the very analytical person I am, it got me thinking about my own marriage and the ratio of good to bad.
Then I started doing calculations in my head. (Yes, sometimes I am obsessive.) Adding up the number of months that I could remember that were especially tough and trying, and comparing them to the really good times. I'll spare you the sordid details of my multiple equations, percents, fractions, and variables all worked out on a piece of scratch paper. It turns out that my marriage was roughly 80% great and 20% not so great. I would've thought that we were closer to about 90% great. It doesn't really matter what the number is, the point is that our good far outweighed our bad. I don't know if we were just lucky, or worked harder than others at maintaining a commitment, or were just better suited for each other and extra compatible, or all of the above. Probably a mixture of all of the above, but that's a whole other equation we won't get into.

We decided early in our marriage that the unit was top priority; never ourselves, or our future children above the marriage. The sum was to be greater than the parts, so to speak. I think that served us well. Not that we didn't have times of being selfish, or petulant temper tantrums of "But, I want...", or focusing on the kids more than us, but the idea of the marriage *first* always brought us back to reprioritizing in our favor when things got kind of squirrely. Marriage is a delicate balance of sacrificing yourself for the good of the whole, but not losing yourself in the process. There is a lot of compromise, picking your battles, and just letting go. And of course a lot of hope that the scale is tipped in your favor and the good outweighs the bad.

So, today I'm feeling thankful that he stuck by my side. Always put me first. Never let me step down from the pedestal he put me on from day one. And that I did all the same for him.

And in the end, the scale was tipped in our favor and we had it pretty good. We had it pretty good...

Tue Dec 7, 2010 | 12:01 PM |
Tick. Tock.

Excerpts from Time, by Sarah McLachlan

Time here,
All but means nothing
Just shadows that move across the wall
They keep me company, but they don't ask of me
They don't say anything at all.
And I need just a little more silence
And I need just a little more time

Time is a funny thing for us grievers. Things that happened right after Andie died seem like years ago to me, that is, if I *even* remember them at all. Just yesterday my brother-in-law reminded me that Andie's whole family had gone to Oklahoma not long after he died to see the extended family. Until my brother-in-law brought it up yesterday, I had completely forgotten that it occurred. And then when I thought about it, I

61

could've *sworn* they took that trip over a year ago- long before Andie died. *And yet*, it seems like just a few months ago that I was giving birth to twins and we were learning about diapers, bottles, and sleep schedules.

There is a time warp around grief that is truly disorienting. I think to the griever, life *literally* stops and then when we "wake up" for a moment or two we see that the world has continued to move on and we have to suddenly catch up. So we end up jumping through time. It reminds me of the book I read in middle school called "A Wrinkle in Time" and the ant on a string illustration. It will take the ant much longer to walk "through time" than if you just put a wrinkle in it and he gets to skip ahead...

Most people's timelines are flat and continuous, and move at a relatively steady pace. But to a griever, there are many wrinkles in our timeline. Times we seem to skip over and move through events at warp speed; so quickly they don't even register in the psyche and leave a trace of memory. Then the timeline smoothes out again and we're back to crawling through time where *every* second seems like it is in the forefront of consciousness.

We widows measure everything by milestones- there are a lot of firsts. The first day, week, month, and year. The first holiday, birthday, anniversary, kid's birthday, our own birthday. The first time to visit that special place, first time we cook his favorite meal, go to his favorite restaurant, hear a special song. The first time we wash the sheets and lose his scent, or the first time we take off the wedding ring. The first time we check the "widowed" box on some form, the first time we have to figure out a new emergency contact on paperwork, the first time we have to answer the "what does your husband do?" question while making small talk. The first Christmas card pictures without him in it. The first time we don't buy his favorite snacks at the store because he's not home to eat them. The first time we make a major life decision on our own without his input, the first time we have to explain it all to our children. The list goes on and on endlessly.

So far I've made it through my own 30th birthday, my kids' 1st birthday, 4th of July, Halloween, Thanksgiving...but I hardly remember any of them. They're all a blur. *Seriously,* how did I manage to get invitations made and plan a birthday party for the twins a mere 6 weeks after he died?

I'm coming up on the 6 month anniversary which seems monumental to me. Half a year without him.

There is simply *NO WAY* that he's been gone that long. More like 6 weeks in my warped existence. I get anxious when I think how much time has already passed because it's going too quickly. Time keeps moving and I don't want it to- and it's taking my girls with it. They are growing and changing too much, too soon, and I feel like I can't savor it. I can't appreciate it because I'm not really here experiencing it all. I'm just going through the motions- I'm merely existing and not *really* living. I try often to be present and engaged, especially with them, but most of the time I'm emotionally drained and simply don't have the energy.

I. Just. Need. More. Time.

But alas, time marches on...

Wed Dec 8, 2010 | 08:56 AM |
I love you...

Excerpts from "I Love You" - by Sarah McLachlan

And I forgot
To tell you
I love you
And the night's
Too long
And cold here
Without you

I grieve in my condition
For I cannot find the words to say I need you so

The night Andie died I didn't tell him I loved him before we went to bed. We said that to each other every night. I'm not sure why we didn't that night; perhaps because we were on vacation and out of our routine, nevertheless, I didn't say it. And he didn't say it to me either.

Then when the chaos started and I knew the situation was serious, I kept telling him that I *needed* him. That the girls needed him. That he had to stay alive because I could not do this without him. But I still did not say that I *loved* him.

It's strange how in the middle of chaos and trauma you can have moments of clarity- a stillness within when thoughts seem to flow calmly and rationally, and the world around you fades away. I remember a moment like this when I had an almost subconscious fleeting thought that if I acknowledged that this might be the last time I said I loved him, then that would make it true. So I didn't say it. It was like I was afraid to jinx myself. That if I actually uttered the words, "I love you, don't leave me" then I was accepting my fate. That if I said it, then that meant that I believed the very thing I could not make myself believe...he wasn't going to make it.

I even had a brief thought about the next day, when I thought it was all going to be okay and he was stable, how I was going to tell him how much he scared me. Admonish him not to ever do that to me again. I was going to tell him that I had been afraid he was going to die. I was going to tell him then how much I loved him.

I was going to tell him then...

Thu Dec 9, 2010 | 02:56 PM |

A Grief Inhabited...

This grief inhabits my soul.
It is a place.
It is a feeling.
It is a state of mind.
It is a virus invading, mutating, and taking over its host.

It controls.
It dominates.
Then it acquiesces.
It grows, changes, and evolves.

It becomes me.
It envelops and surrounds me.
It pushes.
It pulls.
Then it dissipates.

It is a belief.
It is a conviction.
It is a process, a riddle, a puzzle that cannot be solved.
It is me.

This grief...it lives in me.
And I in *it*.

Sat Dec 11, 2010 | 01:55 PM |

Kaleidoscope

My thoughts are like a kaleidoscope. Constantly swirling in my head, one thought seemingly unrelated to the next, yet interwoven and connected, as it is born out of the thought immediately preceding it. What seems like a random assortment of thoughts is really an intricate dance amongst them. One leading, and the next following. With just a subtle shift the thought pattern morphs into something new right before my eyes. The beginning of the word- "kaleid"- sounds like collide. That is my thoughts; colliding with one another and merging together to form something new. Like atoms that collide, bind, and then become a new molecule. My mind is in constant motion these days and often I can't make sense of it. Ending up in a place in my mind and having no idea how I got there. Here's a glimpse into my kaleidoscope...

I stood in the shower today as I let the too hot water beat on my back and inhaled the steam. I thought about how Andie wouldn't have liked the water this hot. I remind myself he is dead. Then I think, how did this happen to me, how am I alone in this, how is he not here? My thoughts jumped to a girl I know who got married not long ago, and how in all likelihood she would still have a husband 6 years and 8 months from now. Why did I not get the privilege of getting past that point? I'm reminded of my wedding day, my joy, my enthusiasm for the future. Had you told me then what would happen would I have continued down the aisle? I think not. I *know* not. This pain would have been too scary. I wouldn't have willingly walked this path; I would not have been strong enough to take this burden on. That's all people tell me these days; how strong I am. I am because I *have* to be, not because I *choose* to be. Had I had the choice I would've been a coward, would have not moved forward down this path. Would've chosen the easier, less painful, path. I would've broken up with Andie had I known that I would lose him. We would've married different people and some *other* young girl would be a widow right now, not me. Then I think that I would not have had my children; other children maybe, some other man's children, but not *my* children. My unique children that only Andie and I could've created together. And I would not give that up for anything now, but had you asked me before it all happened, I would have said other children would be just fine, I would've willingly accepted that fate. Because I would not have known the difference then. That 23 year old girl would not have known that the pain would be outweighed by the gifts. Would not have known the joy and fulfillment that Andie and these babies would bring.

So this experience and all this pain was really worth it in the end- for without it, I would not have my beautiful children, would not have known true love from an amazing man. Then I think, this is why we don't know our futures... it would paralyze us. We would always be making decisions based on what we saw in the crystal ball and changing the course of the future, never knowing what we were really destined for because we messed with destiny. This is why, perhaps I should not consult a psychic or medium to help me get in touch with Andie. What if they know something about my future that would irrevocably change it, if I *too* knew what the future held?

I'm awakened from this marathon of thoughts by the sound of one of the girls babbling as she awakes from her nap. I hear her happy squeals over the sound of the running water in the shower. I turn it off, wondering how long I've stood there lost in thought...and where did this all start in my mind?

This kaleidoscope of thought is my existence. I can't seem to even make sense of things enough to write about them lately. I can't stay focused on a topic. Just lots of thoughts swirling around, constantly shifting and morphing, into something new...

just like a kaleidoscope.

Mon Dec 13, 2010 | 08:57 AM |
Becoming an angel...

Excerpts from "Angel" - by Sarah McLachlan

Spend all your time waiting
For that second chance
For a break that would make it okay
There's always one reason
To feel not good enough
And it's hard at the end of the day
I need some distraction

Oh beautiful release
Memory seeps from my veins
Let me be empty
And weightless and maybe
I'll find some peace tonight
In the arms of an angel
Fly away from here
From this dark cold hotel room
And the endlessness that you fear
You are pulled from the wreckage
Of your silent reverie
You're in the arms of the angel
May you find some comfort there

I have to work really hard to picture Andie as he was alive. To capture the essence of him in a memory that is not overshadowed by my memory of his last moments on this earth. I guess these are snippets of PTSD manifesting themselves; such a horrific flashback to have to relive even for just moments. They hit me at random times. I was struck by this image of him while driving to work this morning, with no idea of what triggered it.

To combat these awful last memories I have to literally push them out of my awareness. I have to conjure specific happy times like how he looked when he walked in the door from work, a smile because he was happy to be home. The boyish grin he had as he laid next to me in bed each night and said he loved me. The embarrassed smile he had when we were driving in the car and he had just danced and acted silly for my benefit. These are the ways I want to remember him. I want to erase the night he died from my memory all together.

I have been wondering lately about the exact moment that his soul left his body; maybe that's why the night he died is at the forefront of my thinking. Exactly when did he become an angel? Wondering if it really happens like it does in the movies where the soul leaves and can look back and see what is still happening here. I know he was gone long before the actual time of death, before that minute printed on the death certificate. I could sense that. But when was the actual crossover? I pray it was not while he was in the back of the ambulance and I was not allowed to be with him...I want to have been there holding his hand when that exact moment occurred. There was a moment before the ambulance arrived when my cousins were doing CPR and I had been holding Andie's hand. I let go for a short second and his hand twitched, as though he was reaching for me. Perhaps that was the moment, his last attempt at connection before he knew we would have no more connection in this physical world.

The question rolls around in my mind and haunts me...exactly when do you become an angel?

Wed Dec 15, 2010 | 11:06 AM |
I win.

People often say that there is a reason for everything. Many times over the years I've wondered the reason for having to lose my father when I was so young. Perhaps the reason I had to lose him was to prepare me for this loss. To guide me through this grief. To allow me to see hope and fulfillment in my future so I may continue to go on living *now*. If losing Andie had been my first experience with tragic loss I would not be coping and functioning very well, and that would prevent me from being a good parent. Because I've walked this walk before, I have some coping skills to draw on and I am able to continue functioning for my girls.

Losing Dad was actually a gift in a way, which even as I type it sounds *INSANE*. But living through that, and working through that has helped me cope with this loss of Andie. Because I have experienced sudden, tragic death before, and come out on the other side still alive and able to find joy, it gives me hope for my future now. I know that I will not only *survive* the loss of Andie, but also thrive and find fulfillment again. Just in a different way than I expected.

I'm different in that regard from other widows who have not experienced loss prior to losing their husbands. Their outlooks are so bleak and they have a hard time believing that it will ever get better. I completely understand where they are coming from because that is how I felt after losing my father. But I don't feel this way about losing Andie because losing my father has taught me many lessons. I have learned how to deal with grief, how to process it, how to accept that while the pain seems unbearable now there is truly a light at the end of the tunnel. I didn't deal well with my father's death; initially I tried to deny it, detach from it, compartmentalize it. It wasn't until 5 years after he died that I finally started to deal with it and got some really good therapy.

I won't make *all* the same mistakes this go 'round as I did with my first bout of grief. I still struggle with the tendency to compartmentalize and detach, but I'm at least aware of these tendencies and can work to combat them. I still want to move through it very quickly and not give the process the time it deserves- so I constantly have to remind myself to slow down and let it be.

But I'm wiser to the process and know what to expect this time. I know that some days will be good and others will be awful. I know that just when I think I'm getting my feet on the ground, grief will throw me a curve ball and knock me back down. The difference is that now I know that I *can* get up.

I can still win the game.
Grief can't defeat me.

Sat Dec 18, 2010 | 02:38 PM |
Settling in...

I visited his grave today as I do on the 18th of every month. It is still mostly just a patch of dirt, tendrils of grass slowly making their way in and blurring the edges, but mostly just still dirt. It looks so fresh and is a visual reminder in the here and now that all of this *is* still so fresh. I sat and watched my tears roll down my nose and land in the dirt. Someone has placed new flowers and a big red bow on his grave. I realized with a sense of irony that the new big red bow is mocking me like it is a present..."open me" it says. Certainly the only present I could ever want is for this to not be my life. For half a second I think about clawing through the earth with my bare hands to get to him. To unwrap my present.

After I left the grave I went to the lake house to water the tree that we planted in his honor. As I sat on the deck overlooking the lake I was aware of the stark contrast between the beautiful, crisp, clear day with the sun warming my shoulders, and the darkness brooding within in me. I sat there listening to the breeze rustling through the trees and the waves lapping against the dock. I begin to cry again. This is exactly the kind of day he loved. If he were here with me now he would be on the lower dock with a fishing pole. I close my eyes and I can see him there- he'd be in his cargo shorts and a sweatshirt. Very likely it would be the exact UT sweatshirt I pulled from his closet and put on today. He'd have his sunglasses and a hat on. I can see him turning around and giving me that wide grin- the very one I see every day in Addison. He'd throw up the universal sign language gesture for "I love you" and I'd smile and do it back. I open my eyes hoping that when I do I will actually see him there, even if it *is* just an apparition. But I do not. So I cry some more.

Today is monumental- it is 6 months today that he has been gone. The full weight of the pain is palpable. I literally feel it in my chest. Today it feels more real than it ever has- the pain is deeper and stronger. I have been very distracted the past few weeks. I can't concentrate or focus, especially in conversation. It's the ol' Charlie Brown, 'wah, wah, wah"...then I have to ask people to repeat things or pretend like I know what they're talking about. I am apathetic, not caring about most things. I want to escape it all. If I'm asked one more time if I'm okay I just might book the next flight to a foreign country and not come back. *Of course* I'm not okay; I just don't want to talk about it because I spend every waking moment thinking about it. The impending holidays and his birthday (the 26th) are ever present in my mind- like vultures circling overhead waiting to poach as soon as I show weakness. I'm giving you all fair warning that thus far it has been the calm before the storm.

I am losing my grip.
I am slipping.
The darkness is settling in...

Sun Dec 19, 2010 | 09:07 PM |
Frayed nerves...

Wow! Single parenting sucks! The girls are in a new phase where almost anything and everything can induce a tantrum...an all out, on the floor, kicking and screaming, tantrum. Furthermore, they outnumber me!

Here's a list of things that have led to a tantrum in the past few days:
Changing a diaper
Sister has a toy I want or is in my general vicinity
I'm hungry and mom can't get food in front of me in the next 30 seconds
A stranger looked at me and waved (No lie, this happened twice in the past week at two different restaurants)
Mom left the room
Mom is on the phone and not giving me her undivided attention
I want Mom to hold me...I don't want Mom to hold me
I don't want to eat what Mom gave me so I will spit it out, throw it on the floor, or better yet rub it in my hair- especially if I just had a bath.

They are so fast and curious; in the time it takes me to change one's diaper the other is into something they shouldn't be into (Christmas presents, Kleenex box, all the DVD's in the cabinet, the toilet, you name it.)

Even laundry is no simple feat. This morning this is how doing laundry went in our house. I go to my room and gather my dirty laundry. I leave the room with hands full, not able to shut the door behind me, and as I'm leaving my bedroom they are crawling in. My bedroom and bathroom are forbidden territory and they know it- when they see an opportunity to cross enemy lines they seize it. I take the clothes to the laundry room and drop it off and go back to get them. In the time it takes me to walk back from the laundry room, one is in my make-up drawer and the other is standing at the tub and has turned the water on. I get them both out of the bathroom and shut my bedroom door behind me. I go back to the laundry room to load the washer. I hear screaming while I'm in there but figure they can fend for themselves for 15 more seconds. I come out and find Addie is eating something out of the fireplace. While I am washing ashes out of her mouth, Allie comes to the kitchen and unloads the entire Tupperware cabinet. After I hastily pick up the Tupperware and throw it haphazardly into the cabinet (gone are the days of the organized cabinet where all pieces have their matching lids) I find Addie tearing up a magazine in the living room. When I take it away she screams, throws herself on the floor, and repeatedly hits my foot- as it happens to be the closest thing to her. Allie crawls around the corner and sees Addie crying so she starts too. After all, the only thing better than one upset child is two. And in this house it is "monkey see, monkey do". Whew- I'm exhausted and it's only 9:30 a.m.!

The only thing they both enjoy no matter what is the bath, and if I could get away with leaving them in the bathtub for 4 hours at a time, I just might. Better yet, maybe I should stay in the bath for 4 hours...

They are draining me in a way they have never drained me before. By the end of the day I have picked them up, put them down, crouched down to clean something up, and picked up toys so many times that my back and neck are achy and sore. Added to the stress and exhaustion of grieving it is all too much. It makes me lose my patience and I react in ways that I never would under different circumstances; yelling and spanking over things that don't deserve such reactions. Then I feel like a horrible parent and my guilt weighs me down even further. It is a vicious cycle. I feel terribly guilty about the little amount of time I get to spend with them (3 hours at most on days I have to work) and I just want to be with them, but then they are so taxing that when I'm with them I just want to be away from them. I am on edge with them, with *myself*, with *everyone*.

My emotions are raw, like live wires and if you come too close you might get shocked.

Tue Dec 21, 2010 | 08:35 PM |

Have yourself a merry little Christmas...

Well, I'm officially out of my funk. No, really I am, *honest*.

I am a pretty optimistic person in general, so it doesn't take me long to start seeing the good side of things. I can't ever hold a grudge, and I can't ever stay in a bad mood for long. Though I did buy a bottle of wine yesterday called "The Pessimist" to drink the next time I'm feeling a little blue! The background text on the label says "half empty" and the description on the back says it is "exactly the kind of wine for selfish consumption". I thought it was cute. I buy wine solely for the name or label...not quite a connoisseur I'll admit, but it's fun that way. Anyway, I divagate... A friend of mine at work and I are always on the hunt for new words. I recently learned that divagate means to digress or ramble on and wanted to be able to use it in a sentence. Ha! I just double digressed...okay, moving on.

Yesterday I went Christmas shopping and really got into the spirit. I was almost giddy buying gifts for the girls and imagining how they're going to react when they get to see all their new stuff that Santa brought. In the evening I went to dinner with my extended family and it was really good to see them all and be a part of conversation that didn't revolve around death/dying/grief/widowhood/etc. and how I was doing/feeling/handling it all. It was great to focus on them and all the neat things going on their lives. I only felt a little melancholy and bittersweet for half a second when my grandfather asked my brother what the score was in the Spurs game, and I thought about how Andie had an app on his phone that kept up with scores in real time and he would've had the answer for my grandfather in about half a second.

Me and the girls had a great day today. We played with a cowboy hat and I got some cute pictures that I've added to the blog. I'm getting excited about going out of town for the holidays. Traveling with the twins is always stressful because there is so much to pack, and so much planning goes into keeping them semi on schedule with meals and naps. But I'm really happy to be leaving town and getting a change of scenery. We are going to stay in my aunt's house in Galveston. We're going to Moody Gardens to see the aquarium and the Festival of Lights. We might even hit the beach if the weather permits, and the girls can see the sand and ocean for the first time. I think the girls are really going to enjoy it, which means that I will by proxy. Anywhoo, it's beginning to look a lot like Christmas around here... and I need to finish wrapping.

Happy Holidays Y'all! And don't forget to have a merry little Christmas in your *own* special way...

Mon Dec 27, 2010 | 02:49 PM |
The art of distraction...

If distraction were an art I'd be right up there with Picasso, Monet, and Rembrandt. I'm really good at distracting myself and staying so busy that I don't have time to focus on the grief. I've figured out that I tend to stay connected to the blogs and hang on every word that other widows say as they are the only ones who truly understand me, and I them. They have become the greatest source of comfort for me. Almost the only source of comfort. I feel bombarded by all the distractions in my "real" life, and when I'm on the blogs I can connect in a different way. I stay so busy with the day to day tasks of life that the only time I really allow myself to think about the grief is when I'm alone in the car, or when I'm on the blogs.

We traveled out of town for the holidays and I purposely didn't take my computer so I wouldn't have ready access to the blog, or facebook, or e-mail. I considered taking my journal but ultimately decided to leave it at home too. I felt like my mind needed a break from writing and processing. I wanted to just *exist* for the holidays. I wrapped myself up in a bubble and screened phone calls and didn't return messages. I just didn't want to talk to *anyone* about *anything*. I wanted to disconnect from the world. I just wanted to *be*. To be with my girls, to be away from my life for a moment, and all that connects me to it. Ironically, I wanted distraction...though in a different way than I am accustomed to.

For the first time in months I truly enjoyed myself. We had a wonderful vacation and I think getting fresh air and a change of scenery, and cutting off all communication with my "real" life helped tremendously. A weight was lifted and I *lived*. I felt joy. I ate good food, I cherished simple things like sunsets on the ocean and the sound of the surf, and my kids' laughter. I was in the moment and connected with my girls like I haven't been able to be for months. We stayed so busy sightseeing and doing activities that I stayed distracted, but in a good way.

The weather was glorious on the 23rd and the 24th so we visited the beach and got some great pictures. The cold front rolled in on Christmas Eve and at about dusk the sky turned a dull gray and the water reflected its color; the point on the horizon where the ocean meets the sky became indistinguishable. For just a moment it seemed that heaven met the earth and I wondered if God was bringing the angels down to meet us. On Christmas night I ventured out to get some milk for the girls and pick up a pizza for us adults. Alone in my car driving along the seawall was almost surreal. I was one of only a few cars on the road. There was a definite sense of calm. A serenity that I crave. The night was pitch black and the moon was covered with clouds so there was no reflection of it glinting off the ocean. Except for some barges and ships way out on the horizon whose lights twinkled, it was just a vast chasm of black. The water and the sky so dark, that again you couldn't distinguish where one stopped and the other began. I guess that's all this life really is...points along a spectrum with no definitive beginning or ending for our souls, despite the fact that our bodies have a definitive start and end point. Our souls just move in and out of this realm and into another, as seamlessly as the ocean meets the sky. And I wondered on this dark night, where was Andie's soul? Was he beside me in the car taking it all in with me, was he back at the house watching over the girls, or was he somewhere out of our reach completely?

The 26th was Andie's 35th birthday and I wanted to celebrate his life that day but I couldn't bring myself to do it. I could hardly acknowledge it, past singing him Happy Birthday with the girls the minute that we all woke up that morning. After that it was a return to the hustle and bustle of packing to go home, and then making the road trip back, unpacking when we got home, then dinner/bath/bedtime routine. And there it was again, distraction.

Sweet distraction seeping back in and working it's magic...

Thu Dec 30, 2010 | 11:47 AM |
Hibernate...

I think the bears are on to something. I want to hibernate. I am over-stimulated, over-saturated, just plain *over* it. Too many people are vying for my time and attention. I know they have good intentions and mostly want to see the girls, not necessarily me- but I'm feeling overwhelmed with trying to keep up with all the obligations. So many friends and family want to get together to do something over the holidays, and all I want to do is stay inside and not speak to anyone. The more people are trying to reach me and connect with me these days the more I want to pull away. Like a turtle retreating into its shell for protection. Like a bear hibernating in the cave until better times come along. I just want to ignore everyone.

Many other widows and most other people are happy about the new year. They are excited to get a "fresh start". To start anew. I feel exactly the opposite. I do not want a new year to come, I do not want a fresh start, I just want my old life back. And the reoccurring theme in my life of time moving too fast is staring me in the face with the countdown to a new year. Once the clock strikes midnight, a whole year is over and a new one is there to face. It's daunting. It's depressing.

I don't want to ring in the new year with celebration- it is gut wrenching for me to think that this year, this *last* year that my husband was alive, this *last* year that my girls were held by their father, this *last* year that everything I've worked for and lived for, will be over. I don't want it all to be over. I don't want to let go of it. I don't want it all to be so final. But, that's what death is-finality at its finest.

From here forward years will be remembered and marked as "after Andie was gone"...no longer the years "*we*" did this or that, but now the years "*I*" will do it all without him. No more "remember when" that includes his name, for now the new memories made will not include him. So this new year is not a reason for me to celebrate or to look forward to ...It's merely one more hurdle in this long race.

So if I don't return your calls, or make plans to see you, or e-mail you back....please forgive me, I'm hibernating.

Sat Jan 1, 2011 | 10:07 AM |
Time capsule...

I've heard it said that your house reflects your state of mind and this is so true for me. I used to be pretty organized and now there is clutter on every surface because I can't focus long enough, or *care* enough to put things in their proper place. My thoughts are jumbled and chaotic- never staying in one place for long. I want to get organized and clear the clutter, but I can't find the energy. The other way this house reflects my state of mind is that I think of Andie all the time, and I haven't changed one thing in this house since he died. Having him on my mind all the time is probably why I don't want to change anything, or maybe because I haven't changed anything is why I think of him all the time. The proverbial chicken or the egg? I don't know. I just can't believe that this is my life- I don't know how this happened to me. So most of the time I pretend that it didn't, that he's going to come home soon, that this is all just a bad dream.

I feel a tension and irritability well up inside me when I'm in this house. I don't feel it when I'm sitting at the lake and I didn't feel it while on vacation, and I wonder if it's a sign that I should start fresh. Close the door on this house and all it holds, and start new. I've considered building a new house on our land, or trying to find a small house on the lake to move to. I mentioned this to Mom and my best friend the other day and they suggested I make some changes here first to see if that makes a difference and helps. Like rearrange furniture, redecorate, paint, etc. There is a visceral reaction deep inside me that is vehemently opposed to this- though I hide that emotion from them at the time. Trying to be reasonable and hear them out.

Later that evening Mom suggests cleaning things out, reorganizing, and maybe giving some of his things away to people who will find them meaningful or useful. I immediately cry when she brings this up- thinking about getting rid of his possessions cuts me to the quick. The thought of changing anything can reduce me to tears faster than almost anything else, which tells me I'm not ready.

The problem is that this house is like my time capsule. I don't want anything to change no matter how small because to move things or get rid of things, especially things that were his would feel like erasing him and I don't want to feel like he didn't exist. I want proof that he was here and left his mark. His hat collection still hangs in the entry hall, his uniform shirts are pressed and hanging in the closet as though he will come home to wear them, his handcuffs, keys, pens, etc. are all where he left them on the valet. I don't even want to throw his shoe polish away though I have absolutely no use for it. It's like anything he touched is sacred. I feel like the only way to truly hold on to him is to live inside the space he inhabited, touch the things he touched, breath the air he breathed, yet...

I want a change. I want a different life somewhere else, not a different life *here*. Because to change things here won't make it better- just different. To get rid of his things or move them won't erase the pain, but I'm afraid it *will* erase the memories. I don't trust my mind to hold the memory of how things were so I want to preserve it all like a time capsule...so I can look back and know that my life with him was real. That I really had him for a time to call mine. That this all isn't an illusion.

I want to leave this place just as it is in my mind, so that when I look back in years to come I can open the time capsule in my mind and nod with comfort to myself,

"Yes, yes...that is how it was. It *all* was true-the good and the bad."

Mon Jan 3, 2011 | 07:48 PM |
Can you hear me?

"Address in the Stars" by Caitlin & Will

I stumbled across your old picture today
I could barely breathe

The moment stopped me cold,
Grabbed me like a thief.
I dialed your number, but you wouldn't be there
I knew the whole time, but it's still not fair
I just wanted to hear your voice,
I just needed to hear your voice.
What do I do with all I need to say?
So much I wanna tell you everyday
Oh it breaks my heart,
I cry these tears in the dark
I write these letters to you,
But they get lost in the blue,
'Cause there's no address in the stars.
Now I'm drivin'
Through the pitch black dark
I'm screaming at the sky
Oh cause it hurts so bad
Everybody tells me
Oh all I need is time
Then the mornin' rolls in
And it hits me again
And that aint nothin' but a lie.
What do I do with all I need to say?
So much I wanna tell you everyday
Oh it breaks my heart,
I cry these tears in the dark
I write these letters to you,
But they get lost in the blue
'Cause there's no address in the stars.
Without you here with me,
I don't know what to do.
I'd give anything
Just to talk to you
Oh it breaks my heart,
Oh it breaks my heart,
But all I can do
Is write these letters to you,
But there's no address in the stars.

Andie,

There is so much I want to say to you and share with you. I talk
to you throughout the day in my head and imagine the things I
think you would say back to me. I carry on these imaginary
conversations and somehow it keeps you alive for at least a little
while, a moment here and there. It seems almost anything can
make you cross my mind. Here's a sampling of how my thoughts
went today.

I miss you. I wish I had been able to dream about you last night.

I got to work and my laptop was stolen over the holidays. I had
to file a police report and when the officer pulled out his little
note pad it made me think of you. I must have a dozen note pads
just like them that you used on duty to write down
tidbits of important information...sometimes I look through
them just to see your handwriting.

Allie stood up on her own yesterday and walked 3 teensy tiny
baby steps- she was so proud of herself. I was so proud of her. I
know you would have been too. Wish you could've seen it.

I've been amazed by the genuine concern that some of your
friends show me. I am so touched when one of them calls or e-
mails to say they have read the blog, are thinking of me, or just
to share how they are doing or what they're feeling. It is so
comforting to know that they have been thinking of you and that
they still haven't forgotten you. I can hear you saying, "Yeah,
he's a pretty good guy"...

I've also been amazed by some of them who are out of touch or
just do the obligatory "check in" text every now and then. I think
it would surprise you to see who is looking out for "your girls"
and who doesn't so much. You would've expected more from
some of them...I'm sad to think of you disappointed.

I've developed a deeper level of respect and admiration for your
brother. He is so good with the girls and I can tell they love him.
They've all developed a very special bond. Watching him play

and interact with them in a fatherly fashion is almost as good as if you were here. *Almost.*

I love you. I wish I still had the last voicemail you left me on my phone. I really just want to *hear* you say you love me.

The car needs air in the tires and has for weeks but I just keep forgetting to do it...you would've taken care of it already. I'm getting better about checking the gas gauge and not letting it get to empty- I think this would make you proud.

These are just a few of the things I think to tell you today, but you probably already knew all this somehow in the realm you now exist in. At least I hope so. I hope that you can hear me and know when I am thinking of you. I hope that you can see all of the wonderful things the girls are doing each day. I choose to believe that you can because what else do I have, really?

So can you hear me? Can you?

Sun Jan 9, 2011 | 09:58 AM |
Signs

I've recently read some books written by mediums describing how our loved ones send us signs from the other side. I've also just finished a book written by another widow chronicling her grief story and the many ways that she received signs from her late husband. So maybe my subconscious mind is primed to be seeing signs, or maybe I'm just more aware of them now that I'm more educated about how to see them.

Nevertheless, I have had several signs come my way in just the past couple of days. A couple of them are slightly obscure and would only mean something to Andie and me, so I won't go into describing those, for it would take way too long to give you all the background information for them to seem relevant. But I will share are some of the more obvious ones.

You may remember my post about a week ago where I discussed my desire to maybe move and start fresh somewhere. My mom and best friend had encouraged me to change some things here before I jumped into such a big decision like building a new house. The advice givers say widows aren't supposed to make big decisions the first year anyway- perhaps I should give myself more time. After that conversation I asked Andie to guide me in the right direction, to help me know what he would have wanted, to basically give me a sign. Should I stay here, build a new house on our land, try to find a house on the lake...?

Well, before Andie died we had been talking with a company that helps you be your own contractor to build a house. We had been trying to set up a meeting with them, but our schedules never jived and we never got around to it. Very shortly after Andie died, the rep from the company called me to follow up and see if we could set up a meeting. I explained to him that since the last time we had talked Andie had passed away and I was just not in a position to even consider building a house...I wasn't even sure at that point if I would be able to afford holding on to our land. I told the rep that I needed some time to think about the big decision and that I would get back in touch with him *if and when* I decided to move. He expressed his condolences and took me off his list of potential clients. I hadn't heard from him since....

Three days ago I was at work and decided that maybe I should call this guy back and set up a consultation meeting just to see what he had to say. I got online to find the number for their office, but then got busy at work and never called him. Later that evening I got a phone call at home. I didn't recognize the number so I didn't answer. Turns out it was the rep from the company. He left a message and said he hadn't heard back from me and just wanted to see how I was doing. I thought it was a strange coincidence that just hours earlier I had been thinking about calling him but never got around to it. Later that evening I checked my e-mail and he had also emailed me.
He asked how I was doing and said he understood the holidays had probably been rough and just wanted to check on me. I

responded to his e-mail and told him that it was such a coincidence he had made contact because I had meant to call him earlier in the afternoon. I told him that I was interested in coming to one of their seminars or setting up a meeting with him to get some specifics on home building, and see if this was even feasible for me.

Over the next day, I started second guessing myself. Wondering what was I thinking? Building a house is a ton of work, especially when you do it yourself. Where was I going to find the time to devote to overseeing a project of that magnitude, and where would I find the money to build the house I really wanted? All of these doubts were flooding in and I started to think that there was no way I should consider building this house on my own.

Then, the guy e-mails me back. He says I couldn't have picked a better time to want to come to a seminar because the next one they are having is in 2 weeks and the guest speaker who will be discussing her experience is a single mother who was widowed after her husband was in a motorcycle accident. She will share her experience of building a home by herself, and then after the meeting she is opening her home up for a tour. I couldn't help but think that if she could do it, I could do it too.

And maybe, *just maybe,* this was Andie's way of sending me a sign. Or was it just a coincidence that the very day I had thought to call this company that the rep called me? Then when I had doubts, he made it all the more clear and gave me a second sign that was almost a direct answer to my doubts. Here was another widow on a similar journey. Was it Andie's way of saying, "You can do this babe"? I believe in you. *You* just need to believe in you. Push yourself." Do I want to push myself in this direction because building this house was *our* dream together and I don't want to let one more part of us die? Or is this the path I'm supposed to take?

Signs...am I choosing to believe the signs because they are pointing me in the direction I *think* I want to go? If they were pointing in a different direction would I choose not to heed them- would I even see them at all? Are they really signs or just simple coincidences that I'm rationalizing (which I'm pretty damn good at) as signs because they are telling me to do what I *want* to do?

Oprah says, "Coincidence is God working in your life" Maybe. Maybe not.
What it boils down to is choice...whatever we believe is of our own choosing.
If I want them to be signs from Andie then they are...

Mon Jan 10, 2011 | 11:43 AM |
Balance Beam...

I realize that all of my relationships are very one-sided right now. They should be reciprocal but they're not. I've never been great at reaching out and making an effort to stay connected with people, but right now it's worse-it's just more than I can handle. It takes all of my mental energy to just exist and I don't have the ability to *think* about connecting with others, much less actually follow through.

It's like when you're a little kid learning how to walk on a balance beam. Each step precarious and requiring great effort. One little distraction that breaks your concentration sends you tumbling and you've lost your balance. After giving birth to two children at one time my equilibrium was off for a while. My focus was on learning how to incorporate two humans into my life who depended solely on me and my husband to exist. Just when I was back on my feet I lost my husband and once again I've lost my balance. Now those two little humans depend solely on me and me alone. My confidence has been shaken, and I have to focus and concentrate very hard to just make it through the day. Each step, no matter how small, is scary. One little distraction and I go tumbling...

I know I'm pushing people away, or at the very least not pulling them in my direction. I don't want people to forget about me. I don't want people to forget about Andie. I don't want people to quit talking about him, or sharing things about him. Now that I'm on the back side of a year, past the first 6 months, and this is no longer considered "new" or "fresh" by most standards, I'm terrified that people will forget. I don't want people to stop checking in or making the effort, but I also understand it's hard to be on the giving end all of the time...

I wonder if this is why the theme of losing old friends and making new ones is so big in the widow world; lots of widows talk about how the very people they thought they could depend on are suddenly nowhere to be found. We simply don't have the mental energy to devote to keeping up with friends, and I wonder if they fade away because they get tired of making all the effort. Because they don't understand that they are requiring too much from us. Because just when things are getting back to normal for them, our lives are hit with the full gravity of the situation just as the shock has worn off. Yet, there are those who *never* give up and keep checking in. I truly thank God for them, and am blessed to have many people like this in my life. I'm just terrified that they too will eventually tire of shouldering all the responsibility to keep our connection going.

I guess what I'm trying to say is...I promise I'll get my balance back. I'm working on it. Just *please*; don't give up on me...

Tue Jan 11, 2011 | 08:55 PM |
Blindsided...

Allie had a follow up appointment with the dermatologist today to look at her birth mark. The clinic where he sees her is in downtown San Antonio- a place I venture only occasionally. On our way home, the usual route, I see graffiti on a wall that I've never seen. The reason I've never seen it is because usually at this point in our drive home I was always on the phone to Andie to tell him how the appointment went, only *this time* I didn't have him to call.

I wasn't on autopilot while talking on the phone like usual; this time I was completely aware of my surroundings. Hyper-aware. *So* aware of all the details I had previously failed to see that it was all grossly unfamiliar. Suddenly I was in a different world. A place I didn't recognize, and for half a second I actually thought I had taken a wrong turn and was lost. It was disorienting and just one more reminder of how his absence impacts me in ways I never would've imagined. Ways I can never prepare for because they hit me out of nowhere. These moments blindside me.

Here I was thinking that the past few days had been going pretty okay. I hadn't been feeling *too* sad so maybe I was hitting the "acceptance" stage. Just maybe, I had finally convinced myself that I could acknowledge that this is permanent. That I've developed a new normal and this is just the way it is now. Just when I was starting to think that maybe I'll actually get through this...

I am blindsided once more.

Grief scores again and takes the lead...

Thu Jan 13, 2011 | 10:57 AM |
Glutton for punishment...

Last night I cleaned off the dresser in our bedroom. All of the sympathy cards that were in a pile, all of the newspaper articles about his death, the flags draped over his casket, the little mementos gathered over the past several months. I boxed up all the cards and newspapers and things I wanted to save. The flags are still folded and on the dresser. But everything else was put away. Surprisingly, it wasn't as hard as I thought it would be. I had been dreading this task and defiantly refusing to do it for so long- as usual, the anticipation of the event was worse than the reality. Mom was there to lend moral support, which helped a great deal.

Mom told me that she was listening to a CD in her car the other day and one of the songs from me and Andie's wedding came on and she had to stop listening to the CD because it made her so sad. I'm the exact opposite- I like to listen to songs that remind me of Andie.

In fact, I have created a "soundtrack" to my life with Andie. There are over 30 songs on it and I continually add more. The songs all hold special meaning and remind me of different times in our life from the start of our friendship, through dating, marriage, kids, his death, my grieving, etc. Some of the songs are really happy. Like the ones that remind me of when we were dating and hanging out at bars on the square of San Marcos during our college days. And of course our wedding songs. Songs that remind me of the drives we'd take through the hill country on sunny days early in our marriage dreaming about where we'd love to buy land and settle down. There is one that reminds me of the last time we spontaneously (rarely happens with twins) "re-consummated" our marriage...I had been cooking one of his favorite meals for dinner and was listening to my iPod in the kitchen. He came into the kitchen and danced with me for a few seconds- a rarity in itself. Then we both started acting goofy, laughed at ourselves, kissed, then...well, you know the rest of the story. These cherished memories are sacred glimpses into how we were when no one was looking and we just had the comfort of each other. One of the songs reminds me of the triumphs over the difficult times in our marriage; how we continued to persevere and made it through and our commitment was stronger for it. The songs that we played at his funeral are on there, and some other songs about losing someone you love. Some of his favorite songs that he would turn up and sing to every time they came on the radio are on there. This playlist is basically the story of my life...of *our* life together. The good, the bad, the easy times, the hard times, the fun we had and didn't have, the daily grind of life...all of it.

Anyway, I listen to this playlist most days in the car on my way to work and on my way home. Sometimes it brings me comfort and makes me smile. Most times it is heart-wrenching and makes me cry. I tell Mom about this last night after she shares her experience of the song making her sad, and she says she can't understand how I can possibly put myself through that. I wonder the same thing and come to the conclusion that it's cathartic. It makes me face the grief full on. It floods my mind with memories of him and though painful, it is also strangely comforting.

I guess I force myself to do these painful things like look at sympathy cards and listen to sad songs because the alternative is to feel numb. Hurting is better than not feeling anything at all-though I never understood that view point until I was put in this position. Most days I'm still so detached and in denial that I'm walking around in a fog. Can you actually still be in denial if you acknowledge that you're in denial? Probably not, so I guess what I am is: bewildered, dumbfounded, in utter disbelief that my husband is *never* going to walk through that door again and give me that "I'm so glad to be home" smile. He is still so *real* to me. My mind can't make sense of all of this.

So why do I push myself to confront the painful stuff when I could just as easily avoid it and stay in the comfort of my fog?

Well, because as the saying goes
It just hurts so good...

Sat Jan 15, 2011 | 09:18 PM |
Note to self: read the fine print...

Today at snack time I feed the girls at the table and the monotony of the task hits me. It feels like I have prepared their meals, fed them, and cleaned up after them all by myself a million times. Then I realize that I have. They were still in high chairs with trays when he died. They were still eating pureed foods and drinking out of a bottle. So much has changed that he does not know about. In the few short months that he's been gone, our lives have dramatically changed in a myriad of small but significant ways. I ponder all the things he never got to see and doesn't know about.

He does not know that:

They can eat with a fork and drink out of sippy cup, all the while eating table food exclusively- no more pureeing veggies
They can hop like a bunny, moo like a cow, and hoot like an owl
They have natural rhythm and love to dance just like me
They love pizza as much as I do
They are able to identify with startling accuracy almost all of the animals, shapes, and many objects in their books, which they look through incessantly
They love each other and often hug and cuddle- their bond is unique and special
They know him; they recognize him in most pictures they see
They love to brush their teeth
They know how old they are and proudly raise their index finger when asked
They love to ride in the car and get excited repeating "Go" over and over when we say we are going somewhere
They give high fives and make silly faces on command
They crawl on everything, and open everything....*everything*
They follow simple commands and directions
They try to put their own shoes and socks on, and at bath time try to take their pants off
They build towers out of blocks and are able to do simple big board puzzles
They love to flip the light switches on and off
They love to eat ice like him, and when they see an adult drinking out of a cup they say "ice" over and over until they are given a piece
They love to rough house and get tickles, something I always imagined him doing with them
They squeal with delight and clap whenever they are proud of something they have accomplished

All of these beautiful, unique things that make them who they are and he has never experienced them. He's never had the joy of seeing them giggle with delight when being chased. Never seen them hug and kiss each other. Never watched with amazement as I have when they aren't sure how to do something and they just keep trying until they get it right. He's never walked into their room at night while they are wide awake, only to have them pretend to be asleep as though they can fool us. He's never had them cling to his leg and demand "up" because they so desperately want to be held.

It is with penetrating sadness that I realize this is all only the tip of the iceberg. He never got to be a part of shaping who they are, and who they will become. The sole task of instilling values, morals, life lessons, and personality traits is left to me.

When I said "til death do us part" this isn't what I had in mind.

This isn't what I signed up for. I sit here heaving and sobbing, asking God if there is any way I can re-negotiate the contract.

Surely, there is an escape clause in the fine print somewhere.

Then I realize, this *IS* the fine print...I just didn't read it.

{PART THREE}

HEALING...

Blessed are those who mourn, for they shall be comforted.
Matthew 5:4 ESV

Mon Jan 17, 2011 | 10:10 PM |
Make a choice...

Today the weather was beautiful for the first time in what seems like forever. I had the urge to get outside and move. To breathe. To feel the sun. To feel *alive*. I haven't been exercising since Andie died but today I *needed* to run. I had the itch. I loaded the girls in the stroller and off we went. The sun was shining but it was still a chilly day. I wasn't able to run as far as I used to. My body hasn't been use to that kind of abuse lately.

As I ran, Andie's ring which is on a chain around my neck, bounced up and down on my chest, stinging my skin. The cold air burned my lungs and my chest tightened. My muscles tensed and strained with the weight of the girls. I wasn't acclimated to the cool weather and it took a minute for my body to loosen up and give in to the pressure. I wondered if this was how he felt when we went running and he complained that he couldn't catch his breath and his chest hurt. I push this thought from my mind. I push the girls up the next hill. I push myself to keep going. This moment is not about him, I tell myself. Every other moment of every other day is about him. But *this* moment, on *this* day is mine. Right now it is about me.

It's about pushing myself to take my life back. To not be defined wholly by the fact that I am his widow. It's about living in the moment and accepting it for what it is. Not wishing it was something different. It's surrendering to the fact that I don't know what tomorrow holds, or the next day, or the day after that- but it doesn't really matter anyway. What matters is being present and engaged with my children, being true to myself, accepting the blessing of being alive-*right now*.

Lately, I've been thinking a lot about creating an acronym for my mantra..."push." I've come up with many but none of them ring true to me. I tossed around...

Sometimes in life, Pretty Ugly Shit Happens (too pessimistic)

Persistence, Understanding, Survival, Hope (not bad, but still not the true essence of what push means to me)

Pain, Undone, Sadness, Heartache (blah, too depressing)

Prayer, Unity, Salvation, Healing (too sappy and idealistic)

And the list goes on and on…

The one that I keep coming back to time and time again because it conveys what push means to me in those moments when I *have* to push myself is:

"Perseverance Unleashed, Strength Harnessed"

Because for me, in the moments when I need a push it's about unleashing the power within myself in order to persevere. It's about harnessing emotional, physical, and spiritual strength to survive.

So today I made a choice. Today I pushed.

Tue Jan 18, 2011 | 01:11 PM |
Word play…

Yesterday at the grocery store I handed the cashier my coupon. She was a young, pretty girl- probably no more than 20 years old if I'm being generous. She noticed my wedding ring, complimented me on it, and asked to see it again. I obliged her though I could feel the anxiety rising…I knew the questions were about to start rolling off her tongue. She oohed and aahed over how pretty it is and asked if he had picked it out himself. I replied simply, saying he had- offering no other details. "He must have really good taste in jewelry," she said. "Yes he does," I reply. Choosing to refer to him in the present tense because that is easier than explaining that he "did" have good taste in jewelry, that he "used to", that he doesn't anymore because he is dead.

She continued to gush about how she and her boyfriend just recently went ring shopping and she was so excited....blah, blah, blah. Honestly I didn't hear another word she said. I was lost in my own thoughts by then.

It was the first time since all of this began that I actually wished I hadn't worn my ring. Not because I'm not proud of it, but because sometimes it's just easier to not have a reason to talk about my husband. Sometimes I don't want to do all the explanations and occasionally I find myself making a split second decision about whether or not to let someone believe my husband is still alive, or jarring them with reality and telling them the truth.

Ironically, this young cashier is the same one who many weeks ago noticed the necklace I wear with a replica of his sheriff's badge on it. In that interaction she asks where my husband works and I awkwardly stumble through the explanation that he used to work at Guadalupe County Sheriff's office but doesn't anymore because he passed away. She gave me the "I'm so sorry I asked" look and profusely apologized. To which I profusely apologized to her for making her uncomfortable. We both pretty much abruptly stopped talking to each other, and avoided each other's gaze through the awkward silence of the guy bagging my groceries. Though she obviously doesn't remember this interaction as she continues to talk about rings, and how lucky I am to have a husband who has such great taste in jewelry. This wide-eyed, young girl, so in love, would be shocked to know what *real* life can do to you.

So I referred to him in the present tense. Letting her (and me) believe for a second that I was going home with my groceries to the man with "great taste in jewelry". Letting her believe in happily ever after. No need to ruin her dreams. No reason to let reality come crashing down around her just because misery loves company.

I was her once. Excited and eager about sharing my future with the love of my life. I was young and in love, and didn't know that it could all slip from my grasp so quickly and stealthily that it would leave my head spinning and my heart empty without the slightest warning.

He has been gone 7 months today. But I guess he still has great taste in jewelry.

Yes, he does…

Wed Jan 19, 2011 | 03:49 PM |
Buttress…

but·tress [buh-tris]
—noun
1. any external prop or support built to steady a structure by opposing its outward thrusts

—verb (used with object)
2. to support by a buttress; prop up.
3. to give encouragement or support to (a person, plan, etc.).

I have my own buttresses in the form of some very important friends in my life. Every 18th of the month we get together for dinner as a way to get my mind off of the sad emotions of the anniversary. Not all of us are able to make it every time being that there are kids/spouses/jobs/ etc. to tend to, but there is usually no less than 4 of us. I look forward to this day the whole month and am always sad when the night has to end. They all bring a unique perspective to my life and understand me in a unique way. There is:

"The other half of my brain" –She thinks like me, knows how I tick, and gets me in a way that nobody else does. We can finish each other's sentences or know what the other one is thinking with a simple look. She is the sister I never had. She has been there with me every step of the way, and no matter how small or slow I might be stepping- she's behind me 100%. She epitomizes what a true friend is. I don't know how I'll ever live up to her example.

"My sister in-law"- she understands the family dynamics from the inside out. She knows the wonderful joys, and sometimes frustrations of being part of such a close knit family. She is one of the most patient and giving people I know...and she can *always* make me laugh!

"My light"- she is always in a good mood, kind to everyone she meets, and a true inspiration with her gentle, caring soul. I want to have a disposition like hers. I want to make everyone I come in contact with feel special, and worthy, and awesome like she does.

"The straight shooter"- the only other single mom in the group, she understands the tribulations of flying solo. She really gets what it's like to not be overwhelmingly happy for others who are getting married/having a baby/in a new relationship, etc. because we know that life just isn't *always* so grand. She keeps me grounded and has great perspective; never letting me get worked up over the small stuff.

"My fireman"-You know that fireman saying that they "run in when everyone else runs out"? Well, when everyone else ran out she ran in... okay, not *everyone* else ran out, but she is the happy surprise in all of this. Someone who has become closer to me through this because she stepped in and wasn't afraid to do so. She didn't avoid me like some people have. She was the casual friend who has become a true, close friend. I'm so thankful for people like her and for her courage- something I admire.

"The cheerleader" - She's been my biggest cheerleader for writing a book about my grief and using the experience for good. Always ready to lend a hand with offers of help and support. And *never* afraid to tell it like it is and give me her honest opinion.

"The seen it *all* from the beginning friend" - married to my husband's best friend, she has been around me the longest and knew Andie and I both before we were a couple. She is the only one to have known us as a couple for the entire time we were together. She knows the *full* history.

All of them give me something I need, and I can only hope that in some small way I am able to return the favor for them. They fulfill me, sustain me, prop me up, and support me...

Being an introvert, I've never been one to form lots of friendships. I remember in middle school when cliques and being left out was commonplace. I took on the stance that I didn't need friends. I was perfectly happy being alone. And for the most part I was, and still am. But I distinctly remember a heart-to-heart talk with my father during that time in which he said, "Brooke, you need people. You can't go through life alone." And he was right.

I thank God for these wonderful angels that have been put in my path to help me learn that lesson once again. I do need people. I need *them*.

Fri Jan 21, 2011 | 03:39 PM |
3 days later...

The healing is creeping in. Ever so slowly. As though all the crying I do is wringing out the pain from my soul and tear by tear, drop by drop, it is making room for peace to soak back in and settle in its place.

I know this because I forgot to go to the grave this month. I go on the 18th of every month without fail. It has been so important for me to do this that I make special arrangements to be able to go. Getting up early so I have time to go before work, or asking the nanny to stay a little late so I can make a detour there on my way home from work. But this month, it didn't consume me. This month, I simply forgot. It didn't even cross my mind.

Until today... 3 days later.

Sun Jan 23, 2011 | 08:22 PM |
Enough

Allie got sick today. I think she'd been working up to this for a few days. She'd been fussy and not sleeping well and I couldn't really figure out what was wrong. Today she made it abundantly clear exactly what was wrong.

After church we went to a restaurant for lunch and before we could even be sat at our table she vomited all over me, all over herself, all over the bench in the waiting area. My father in-law ended up having to drive us home so I could bathe her and get her in bed. I had to ask my father in-law to stay with me and feed Addie lunch while I got Allie and myself cleaned up.

A couple of hours later we went for round two and she threw up all over me in the recliner. She remained lethargic all day. Not taking any fluids and just wanting to be held. Addie still had to be cared for and I couldn't drop everything for Allie's sake and just let Addie suffer. So my in-laws stayed with me all afternoon and until I got the girls in bed tonight. I literally *could not* have made it through the afternoon without them.

And it's not until now, in the quiet and calm of the evening when I am once again alone that the tears come. Because I realize I simply cannot do it all. Because I shouldn't have to rely on my in-laws to sacrifice their entire day to help me. I should have a husband here, who though he would gag at the smell of their vomit, would be in the midst of it all with me. Who would be yelling at me from the kitchen while I'm bathing Allie, "Babe, what am I supposed to feed Addie for lunch?" And I'd yell back, "Give her a hotdog, a cheese stick, and some fruit." And then roll my eyes to myself that he couldn't think of a simple lunch to put together while I am busy washing the chunks of vomit from my daughter. And when she vomited in his favorite recliner he would be disgusted and want to spray it with Lysol. I'd tell him to put her clothes in the washer and he would, but he wouldn't know to rinse the vomit in the sink first and I'd be annoyed again. He would've wanted to be helpful so he would've gone out and picked us up dinner, cleaned up the kitchen, picked up the toy room, fed the dogs, and taken out the trash, all without me asking. Then he would've held those babies tight and cuddled them til they fell asleep in his arms, all the while, telling me to go take a shower, knowing I would need the 20 minutes to myself.

I want him to be here so I can be annoyed at the little things again. So I could have someone who knows me so well that I wouldn't have to tell him what I want from the fast food restaurant, he would just know. I want him here so I can crawl into bed at the end of this night, sigh, and chuckle with him about how crazy he was to spray the furniture with Lysol. I would kiss him and tell him that I loved him and that I really appreciated all his help today. He would've said, "But all I did was make a hotdog."

And that would have been enough...

Tue Jan 25, 2011 | 04:02 PM |
Adrift...

I've been feeling adrift, floating around with nothing tethering me down. No one to anchor me. I feel myself grasping for connection with others yet it always leaves me unfulfilled. As people continue to move on with their lives and I become less central to their focus, I feel starved for attention. More disconnected than ever. I'm checking e-mail and the blogs more often- hoping there will be a gift in my in-box or a new post someone has put up that will validate me. But *nothing* fills the emptiness.

The only one who could really be the connection I always needed and wanted is gone. Nobody gets me as well as he did. I will never find another who needs me the way he did. I will never want to be with someone as much as I wanted to be with him; he was just so comfortable to be with. He made it all okay. He gave me purpose. He anchored me and gave me a direction to follow. Now my line has been cut and I'm floating without direction because there is no one to guide me.

I never believed in soul mates when he was alive. I always believed that there were several people we could come across in our life paths who we could settle down and make a happy connection with. I believed that it all had to do with timing, and if each person was ready at the right time then it would work. Most of the time I still believe that, but more and more these days, as I feel adrift and like nobody gets me the way he did, I entertain the idea that perhaps he *was* my soul mate. My one and only.

Nobody can fill the void. Nobody leaves me satiated.

I'm always clinging and wanting more, and what I realize is that I just want more of *him*.

Wed Jan 26, 2011 | 01:55 PM |
Beautiful in his eyes...

I was updating the apps on my phone today, something I hadn't done in ages. Some of them were ones that Andie had put on his phone and when I combined our plan together, his apps became mine. Since they were tied to his account it wanted his password to perform some of the updates. I tried several passwords that I thought it might have been, but none worked and it asked me if I would like to change the password. It said I could answer the security questions that Andie had set up or have a new password sent to his e-mail account. I figured I had a pretty good chance of being able to answer the security questions correctly so I proceeded with that option. First it asked me for his date of birth. This is going to be easy, I thought. Then the second question appeared:

"Who is beautiful?"

I entered my name and "presto!" - I had instant access his account. I thought it was so sweet that he had set this up as his security question. It literally made my heart smile and brought a moment of pure joy that I haven't felt in over 7 months. I've never doubted his love for me, but in that moment it was affirmed so strongly. He was always thinking of me in all that he said and did. He never saw me as anything but beautiful; even after the ravages of pregnancy and childbirth when I became the most insecure about myself. And even after he is gone I still have these little affirmations to reassure me since he can't actually reassure me himself anymore.

Seeing that question pop up today was almost as good as hearing him actually say the words himself.

I was always beautiful in his eyes.

Mon Jan 31, 2011 | 12:53 AM |
Knowing...

I'm lying awake feeling like I'm going to vomit with a flutter in my chest that can only be described as the beginnings of a panic attack. I've just had a flashback of the night Andie died and can't go back to sleep.

I'm trying to think what triggered this tonight and it must have been a conversation I had with my mom earlier in the weekend. I told her that I had known Andie was not going to make it before the ambulance even got there. She was surprised that I had never shared this with her; she too knew he wasn't going to make it then, but had never shared that with me. I've never spoken it to anyone really because to admit it feels like I gave up hope somehow. It's the same reason I couldn't tell him I loved him that night- It was like admitting defeat if I told him I loved him for what I instinctively knew would be the last time. And that by somehow doing that, I would be the one to seal his fate. Not a responsibility I was willing to accept. So I held out a tiny sliver of hope, but something deep inside me just *knew*...

So tonight the flashback is about that night and me trying to figure out the exact moment when I knew that he was going to die. Replaying it moment by moment to see if I can pinpoint when the "knowing" came. I don't recall having a conscious thought that he was going to die but I knew it on an intuitive level. It was purely gut instinct, but I knew. It washed over me at some point. I remember when we finally got in the ambulance and I thought I should pray, but for a split second I wondered if it was worth it because I knew it wouldn't make a difference. I was already angered with God and feeling resigned to the fact that he wasn't going to help me...though that too was not a conscious thought. Just a feeling deep inside...but I prayed anyway holding on to that tiny sliver of hope because my mind could not accept what my instinct already knew.

I had the same gut level sense of "knowing" the day I learned my father died. I had gone to school like a regular morning that day. The few days prior my dad had been having some heart problems but the doctors had sent him home- everything was going to be okay. The assistant principal came up to me in the cafeteria and told me to go get my things because my mom was coming to get me...in that moment, though no other details were given to me, I knew my dad was gone. Again, I didn't have the conscious thought that he was dead but I intuitively sensed it.

It's a feeling of deep foreboding that comes with this sense of knowing. It's painful, gut-wrenching, and literally heavy. It's something that is very hard to even put into words. It's intuitive, instinctual, primal. There is a millisecond of extreme focus and peaceful acceptance of fate when the "knowing" creeps in but then your mind takes over again, trying to will it all to be different, fighting to make the *impossible* possible.

Your mind is the last to catch up, but your body knows, your soul knows.
Your heart knows...

Tue Feb 1, 2011 | 08:47 AM |
Thanks for the sunshine...

Today the cold rolled back in to Texas. The past few days have been unseasonably warm. Yesterday was 78 degrees and I took a jog with the girls and enjoyed the sunshine. This song came on my iPod while we were out and it made me think of Andie. He knew how much I hate the cold and I imagined him sending me a little extra burst of sunshine yesterday just to brighten my day.

Excerpts from "Somewhere Down in Texas" by Jason Boland

In a place that big, a man could get lost
Never mind the time, forget about the cost.
There's more important things.
She's somewhere smiling north of San Antone.
I've got her number but I stare at the phone.
Cause I still want to believe.
Cause no matter how big the storms I know I can find me a
place that's warm.
The sun is shining somewhere in Texas.
I hope it's shining on her
Somewhere down in Texas.

I got the sunshine you sent yesterday babe!

Fri Feb 4, 2011 | 08:16 PM |
Cheated

It snowed today. In Texas! The girls will likely not see this happen again for another 15-20 years so we took advantage of the opportunity and let them play in the snow. They had fun for about 10 minutes and then got bored, and I got cold. Inside we went....

We decided to make cupcakes because the girls turned 18 months old today. It was their 1 1/2 year birthday so we decided to celebrate...that was Grandma's great idea. They even got to help make the cupcakes- such big girls!

Of course, the best part was getting to eat the cupcakes! They each got 2...most of it ending up on their laps and the floor, but it sure was fun! And they smelled like icing for the rest of the afternoon!

While they were napping I came across an old picture of Andie and me. It was taken just a few months after we got engaged when we thought we had our whole lives ahead of us, and it made me really sad... it reminded me of how little time we actually had together. I started reminiscing and trying to figure out exactly how long he was part of my life. He kissed me for the first time on April 11, 2001- I remember it like it was yesterday and then I realized he was not even "mine" for a whole decade.

He was part of my life and my good friend since I was 19, but not *truly* mine for a whole decade and I'm left feeling so cheated. I cry in the shower thinking of how little time we had and absent-mindedly draw a heart in the condensation on the shower door. Almost as quick as I can draw it the water drips and blurs the lines making it almost indistinguishable. I draw it again. As quick as I finish drawing it, it vanishes before my eyes- just like our time together. I'm left feeling like what we had was nothing but a mirage. Something you think you see, but it's not quite tangible, and the closer you get to it the more you wonder if it was real at all. It just seems like he slipped through my fingers...It all went by so fast.

Drawing the heart on the shower door reminds me of the times when one of us would write a little love note in the steam on the mirror while the other was in the shower. And the time years ago when he left dozens of post-it notes around my apartment on which he'd written "I love you". He hid them in places so I was finding them for weeks...my linen closet, the pantry, the junk drawer, the medicine cabinet...they were everywhere. I saved them all for a while, but years later I eventually threw them away thinking that a pile of random post-it notes wasn't very meaningful after all those years in comparison to all the other love notes and cards he had given me. I'd give anything for that stack of post-it notes today. For a simple love note in the steam on the mirror when I get out of the shower. For one more tangible thing...just a simple thing to prove that it was all real.

Anyway, it wasn't a horrible day, it wasn't a great day...just one in which I constantly had a feeling that he was missing out on so much. The first time for the girls to see snow. The fun we had making and eating cupcakes to celebrate their "half birthday". The mundane and simple moments shared with the girls, many of which happen every day.

I just feel like I got cheated. More than that, the girls got cheated. He got cheated. Like we weren't told the rules of the game before we agreed to play.

And there is just no way I can make it all right...

Mon Feb 7, 2011 | 08:56 PM |
Therapy

I went to my first "young widows" grief group today, and by young widows they mean under age 55. I was *by far* the youngest widow there and the only one with small children. The other women had teenage or grown children. Some were on their second marriages and had step-children. One lady had been married longer than I've been alive. So I didn't quite feel like I was in the company of my peers, though I realize a 30 year old widow with toddlers is probably quite rare...except that I know so many from the blogging world. I was just hoping that I might find somebody close to home that I could forge a friendship with.

I was in the middle in terms of how far out I was from my loss. The newest was 4 weeks and the longest was 3 years. So again, *not really* in the company of my peers. The newer widows are still in the worst, shocking, painful part...while I have processed some of that and am trying to gain my footing with who I have to become now. I am in the growth and rediscovery stage, which the widows who are farther out have already sort of grasped. The positive side of this is that perhaps we will all have some insights to give each other about the different stages.

The other way I felt very different from the group is that I work in the psychology field. I've racked up a couple of degrees in psychology. It's what I do, it's what I know, it's how I function. Most of the time when I process things with my best friend (also in the psychology field) it's like I'm doing therapy on myself. Using the techniques on myself that I would on a client- then my friend gets her turn at me so I feel like I have a built-in therapeutic support system.

Honestly, in a therapeutic setting it's hard to impress me. It's like playing chess with a really good opponent who is always thinking a step ahead of you...I usually know what's coming and what direction it's going to go. It's hard to counsel the counselor so to speak.

I know all the ins and outs of how therapy is supposed to work. I know the theories and techniques, I know how group therapy dynamics are made and broken, I have the insider's point of view. It's kind of like knowing the secret to a magic trick- it loses its luster when you see the trick performed once you know it's all just sleight of hand.

So today, I felt like I knew what cards the therapist was holding before we even got started. And true to form she followed the script pretty much as I imagined she would. Not to say that it wasn't helpful information, it just wasn't anything I didn't already know. And I had to consciously remind myself to stop my internal dialogue when the other women were talking, to stop diagnosing them in my head and thinking of which way I would handle it if I was the therapist. And those of my psychology friends out there reading this will recognize my stand-by defense mechanisms of rationalization and intellectualizing have reared their ugly heads, and just to keep it interesting I've added a hint of narcissism to the mix. I know I need to get out of my head and deal with some real emotions...that's why I joined the group. So anyway, I didn't walk away feeling enlightened or any more connected to anyone like I had hoped.

Granted, it was only the first session and the basics had to be gotten out of the way. I'm hoping that the next sessions will push my boundaries and force me to allow the therapy to work, and not let me get away with working the therapy.

Wed Feb 9, 2011 | 08:28 AM |
It's all about you...

Something he used to say to me all the time was "It's all about you." Sometimes it was completely sincere, like on my birthday or if he was just feeling particularly sweet he would say "Today is all about you babe. We can do whatever you want to do today." Sometimes if I was being selfish or demanding he would say with a hint of sarcasm, "Oh, today is all about you I see." And it would bring me back to reality and help me realize I needed to think outside myself for the moment. Or if we just couldn't decide what we wanted for dinner he would say, "Whatever you want...it's all about you."

The truth was, to him, it really *was* all about me. I was the center of his world and he let me know it. And he let everyone else know it too; not that he gushed about me to other people all the time, but you could tell by the way he looked at me, by the way he respected me, and by the way he treated me. One of the most treasured conversations I've had since he's been gone was with one of his really good friends from work. He called me a few days after Andie died and cried on the phone with me. He told me how much I meant to Andie, that I was his whole world, that he loved me more than anything, and he talked about me all the time. This friend even said he hoped that he and his wife could have the kind of love that Andie and I had. What we had was *that* good...it was something that others envied and wanted to emulate.

Even though to Andie it was always all about me, I felt the same for him. I made decisions based on what I thought would make him happy. We placed each other before ourselves and I believe that is what made our relationship so strong. We always wanted to please each other and do things that would make the other happy. Self-sacrificing for the greater good of the marriage. It wasn't something we talked about, we just did it. We put each other first. So while he felt it was all about me...it really was all about him in my eyes. I feel so very grateful to have been able to experience love and commitment like we had. I don't think I'll ever be lucky enough to find it again.

A song is what got me thinking about all of this today because I know it's exactly how Andie felt.

But really...
It's *still* all about you babe.

Fri Feb 11, 2011 | 10:41 AM |
Approval ratings...

I don't know if I've always been so concerned with obtaining the approval of others...probably, but it's hard to remember how I was before Andie died. But now the need for approval is magnified. All it takes is one raised eyebrow or comment to send my confidence plummeting and I'm second guessing myself. I've had a really weird week. I haven't been overly emotional or sad, but I have felt very "blah". Others can sense it too. I've been asked several times this week, "Is everything okay? You seem..." I usually cut them off before they can finish the sentence. I plaster on the smile and make up some excuse as to why I look like I'm about to lose it. You know...fake it til you make it!

I haven't blogged much and haven't touched my journal in weeks. There hasn't been much to write about because I'm back in that place of feeling like I've already written about everything that I'm feeling right now, it's all just cycling back around again. Same song, second verse.

Still feeling completely shocked that this is permanent. *Still* missing the comfort of Andie's touch. *Still* wishing he could see how much the girls are growing and changing. *Still* feeling ambivalent about my future. Still wanting to change everything about my life while at the same time wanting to change nothing at all. *Still* amazed at how almost everything I say, do, think, and feel revolves around him or reminds me of him. *Still* feeling like the person I once was died with him, and I'm having to rebuild and redefine who I am. *Still* angry that this new life was forced upon me and not anything I had a choice in. *Still* feeling like I'm right where I started. Just moving in circles and continuing to come back to the same place in this journey over and over again.

Some weird feelings of a strong desire to "move on" have hit me this week. I haven't felt that before, but this week I have this need to abruptly slam the door on this life, dust off my hands, and try to forget it even existed. Then I feel guilty for thinking that way and become very sad and morose.

I've even thought about whether or not I want to date someone. Gasp!! Mainly because I'm so very lonely and I miss the attention and companionship of a man. And I've been reading about other widows who have found love again and have "success" stories- I want to be in *that* club instead of this club. And *mostly* because the topic is starting to come up in conversation with others much more frequently.

Subtle comments and hints from others about "when" not "if" I decide to find someone else are working their way into conversation. A few weeks ago someone even asked me when I'm going to stop wearing my ring. "When I don't feel married anymore," was my response. I feel like others want me to start moving in that direction so then I feel pressured to do so just to make them comfortable- this is where the approval issue comes in. Sometimes I even preemptively joke about it so it's not the proverbial elephant in the room- hoping to alleviate everyone else's discomfort about the question hanging in the air..."When will she move on?"

Wanting to please the world, as if to say, *"See,* I'm grieving the "right" way. I've mourned the requisite amount of time and am moving on in a healthy manner, thank you very much." Trying to strike the perfect balance, neither wallowing in my grief, nor pushing past it too fast. When I actually picture myself with someone else I have a strong urge to vomit, so I know I'm not ready for that.

I *know* I can only do this at my own pace, in my own way, (as most of you will probably comment) but my confidence in everything has been shaken and I'm left just wanting everyone's approval. I'm terrified of making a wrong decision in any aspect of my life. Whether or not to date, whether or not to build a house or move, whether or not to stay in the same career, whether or not to spend money in a frivolous manner by completely redecorating my whole house, whether or not to allow my kids to have one more cupcake after dinner. I don't want to be the girl that everyone whispers about in hushed conversation because they don't agree with the decisions I'm making, or worse yet think I'm absolutely crazy.

I know I shouldn't care what others think, but I do. I can't help it.

I just want my approval ratings to be good...

Fri Feb 18, 2011 | 05:34 PM |
Soul Searching

"You never know how much you really believe anything until its truth or falsehood becomes a matter of life and death to you."– C.S. Lewis in A Grief Observed

Andie has been gone 8 months today and through a lot of reading, research, and deep soul searching, this is what I've come to know.

We all think we know so much about the world and the way it works. But we really don't *truly* know much at all. I was naïve enough to think that I knew happiness, sorrow, joy, and pain in my former life...but what I've come to truly know is that I only understood those things on a fractional and minuscule level, through the hazy perceptions of what had been taught to me or what I had experienced in my relatively easy life. It is through the difficult, bring you to your knees, make you want to die moments that the veil is lifted and you are awakened to what is truly there at the deepest, purest level. This is when the "aha" moment occurs and you finally "get it".

When I use the word "know" I mean at a level that is deep within you, that shakes you to your core, that nobody can reach save for God and maybe yourself. To know with a conviction and with a purpose.

You cannot know light unless you have known darkness.

You cannot know joy unless you have felt despair.
You cannot know gratitude unless you have been in need.
You cannot know love unless you have been alone.
You cannot know comfort unless you have been in pain.
You cannot feel exhilarated unless you have been loathsome.
You cannot find yourself unless you have been lost.
You cannot triumph unless you have failed.
You cannot find strength unless you have been tested.
And I *dare* say...

You cannot know God and have faith in him unless you have had a reason to question him.

If there have been no trials, tribulations, or tragedies in your life to test your faith, then how can you *possibly* know how to call upon that faith? You can't until you have to...up until then it's all theory and conjecture.

The veil has been lifted and I see the world as I've never seen it before. I consider things from a new perspective, believe in things I once doubted, and know things in a way I don't think I could have ever come to understand had I not been forced to go through this process. It's akin to not having a true idea of what parenthood is like until you're in the middle of it. You *think* you know...but you don't *really* know.

Despite the fact that there is a gaping hole, there is a depth and richness to my life that was probably always there but only now am I able to acknowledge it and appreciate it. Though there are questions, there is a deeper spiritual connection. A stronger faith- not only in the existence of a God, but a faith in myself.

There is a sense of knowing; of being privy to information that the rest of the world is not. I feel like I know some of the secrets of the universe now. I value people and relationships more than ever. The focus on career, salary, material things is no longer meaningful. Things that people around me focus on and worry about seem petty and inconsequential, and it is though my heart gets a sly smile as if to say, "if only you knew how important those things are, if only"…

I feel more grounded, more confident. I feel truer to myself than I have ever been. There is a sense of being on the "right" path, though I never knew I was on the wrong path before. I have an inner serenity that I've never felt. My eyes have been opened in a way that I cannot even put into words. I have been enlightened. I get it, I *finally* get it.

I have come to understand that God gives us the negatives so that we can then, and *only* then, truly understand, know, and appreciate the positives by comparison. It is so we can appreciate the difference, because we cannot have one without the other.

"I once was blind, but now I see" - John 9:25

Mon Feb 21, 2011 | 08:40 PM |
Finding my way back…

So I went to my grief counseling group today and one of the things the counselor talked about is how when we grieve our immediate reaction is to try to go back to the past in our minds and relive the good and happy times with the person we lost, rather than moving forward through the death and subsequent grieving process. We do it because that is what's comfortable. And the past is where we'd rather be…with the one we loved and lost. We do this by reliving memories and consciously trying to hold onto the essence of the person.

The mind tries to find its way back to where it wants to be. What I have found though, is that the more I try to remember him and conjure specific memories, the more they elude me. Just as I begin to grasp a memory it slips away and is replaced by my memories of the day he died. My grief counselor says this is normal at first especially if the loss was traumatic, but with time the happy memories come back and often we don't know what triggers them.

Sure enough, this past week I have been flooded with memories that come whenever they see fit. They don't ask my permission. They come and surround me with their comfort. They have been triggered by songs, smells, sounds, and even strangers. I have relished in it this week, but it also brings so many emotions as I have to constantly face the fact that they are just that- memories, and no longer my reality. The sting of disappointment and disbelief is still raw and painful.

I would do anything in this world to be with him again, to find my way back to him. Wishing my life away until the day I meet him in heaven is not above me. But I know that my only realistic option is to keep him alive through my memory so I am desperately trying to grasp onto any and every moment in time we had, no matter how small in the hopes that I just might... find my way back to him.

Wed Feb 23, 2011 | 08:21 AM |
Highs and lows...

Will the highs ever stop being outweighed and interrupted by the lows? This is of course a rhetorical question. The answer is probably never, it might get better, but I suspect there will always be the tinge of bittersweet.

Last night Allie walked on her own for the first time. This is a HUGE milestone for her; she has had some hip problems and has had a very difficult time learning to walk because her hip is rotated and not aligned properly. We've been doing physical therapy and chiropractic adjustments and she has made vast improvements in the past couple of weeks.

Last night I was playing with the girls in their room. We were all having the best time rolling around and rough housing. I was doing a bunch of tickling, just soaking in the sounds of their wonderful laughter. While we were playing Allie stood up and

walked about 5 steps to me all on her own, completely
unsupported. I was so excited and started clapping. Then Addie
started clapping for Allie too, and Allie was so proud of herself.
She did it several more times and we kept playing.

Then I came crashing down when I realized how proud Andie
would be and how excited he would have been to see this
happen. So there I am laying on the girls' bedroom floor
sobbing. Of course they're wondering what the hell just
happened since seconds before we were all giggling.

I managed to pull myself together but was full of tension and
irritability for the rest of the evening. When I finally got myself
to bed the tears came back again. All I can think is... Why? Why
did this ever have to happen? Why me? Why them? Then I got
angry with God, and then I got angry with Andie for leaving.
Irrational, yes- but it's what we grievers do. I cried so hard I had
to remind myself to breath. Big, racking sobs...until I fell asleep.

And that is what life is like in the Simmons household these
days. Highs and lows, laughter and crying, joy and pain.

All cohabitating...

Wed Feb 23, 2011 | 08:53 PM |
The ripple effect...

The irony in all of this is that those who were closest to me
before Andie died are now the ones I find myself having
difficulty relating to. There is a sense of disconnect that has
slowly crept in. I have changed so much that they can no longer
relate to me as the "old" Brooke, and I can no longer relate to
them as the "old" them. I have been forced to evolve into a
different person and they have not. They have not changed and
grown with me and so it seems we have grown apart. The old
expectations they had of who I was, how I would react to things,

how I think about things, is no longer valid and they are left not knowing who I really am anymore. Most days I don't even know who I am anymore, so how could they possibly be expected to know me. They try to interact and relate to me in the same ways as before but it results in a hollow feeling for me. Sometimes it feels forced or contrived. I don't know if they feel it too, or if this is a one-sided observation on my part that we just aren't clicking like we used to.

We are out of step and out of sync. With me being several paces ahead of them in some areas and several paces behind in others, but never quite getting into the right rhythm together. It's not really fair to expect the rest of the world to undergo this growth process with me step by step, but in the end I believe some will get left behind because they aren't keeping pace with me. I find myself nodding my head and smiling in agreement with people, and inside all I can think is, "You just don't get it." But that is through no fault of their own, thank God they can't actually relate to where I'm at- I wouldn't wish this on anyone. This is not a judgment of others, but merely observation of how things have changed in my life.

This is the strange ripple effect of death; it doesn't just take the person who actually dies. It takes all those around the dead person with it, and irrevocably changes who they are and who they will become. The closer you are to the one who dies, the more you are changed. And by extension of that, it changes how all those people relate to each other. But all of this is unspoken and everyone seems to be bewildered and unable to put their finger on what is so different. Nevertheless, it is different. So very different that it's palpable, yet unexplainable.

Strangely I feel at peace with this. It is sad to think of losing friends or people who have been close to me, but I understand that it is probably the natural course of things so I'm not angry or resentful. I'm just aware that it might happen.

I feel like they want to hold onto the "old" me as much as I want to hold on to Andie, but the brutal truth is that the "old" me died with him.

And neither one of us is coming back...

Thu Feb 24, 2011 | 03:34 PM |
Avoidance...

I have put a deadline on myself to do all the stuff around the house that I need to do during my spring break which is coming up in a few weeks. I've been avoiding most of it because it's just been too much to think about, but I think I'll feel a lot better if I get it all accomplished.

My grief counselor calls this "instrumental" grief; grieving through doing tasks or projects. Planning the 5k in honor of Andie is a perfect example of how one "instrumentally grieves" she said. She told me that people who grieve this way tend to be less emotional in their grief- less feelers and more doers, which made me feel less like a freak for not crying all the time like I think I should be doing. I have really felt like there was something wrong with me because I'm not an emotional wreck on most days of the week. Not to say that I don't have crying attacks and days where I feel like I could cry at the drop of a hat, but for the most part I just go about my day feeling wistful and nostalgic, wishing he were still here, but not a blubbering mess.

On the list of things to do:
1. Re-arrange my bedroom and put up a fresh coat of paint.

2. Organize the funeral memorabilia and find a place to store it.

3. Organize my office; file all the paperwork, bills, and forms associated with death. Shred what is no longer needed.

4. File our taxes. I've been avoiding this one since there is a bunch of new stuff to consider this year like the fact that I've received social security income and life insurance, and we have a ton of medical bills related to the night he died that we might be able to deduct. When I got Andie's w-2 in the mail I opened it and it was about half the amount that he usually makes. I almost called the HR department at his company thinking some huge error had been made- then it hit me...He only lived half of the year, only worked half of the year, and therefore only earned half of what he usually did. UGH! Grief bites you in the butt in the strangest ways.

5. Paint the living room.

6. Consider packing up or getting rid of some of Andie's belongings...pretty sure nobody wants to hold onto his underwear and socks for sentimental reasons so that might be a good place to start.

I try to avoid the "in your face" tasks that remind me so clearly that he is gone. And I do pretty well at it most of the time, but I have to start moving forward at least in small measure so I'm doing what I do best: making a list and setting a goal. We'll see how far it gets me.

Sun Feb 27, 2011 | 07:57 AM |
I'm not a single parent...

The first thing I usually do in the morning is check the widow blogs I follow to see how everyone is doing. It usually helps me get through the day feeling not so isolated in my experience of the world right now.

This morning I read one and it resonated with me. Especially the part where she made the distinction between being an "only parent, not just a single one".

I've tried to rationalize my plight to myself by telling myself there are a million single parents out there and if they can do it, so can I. But it's never really quelled my frustrations with doing this alone. And here's why: I am the *ONLY* one who will ever kiss a boo-boo, clap at their school play, get on them for bad grades, talk to them about their first boyfriends, hug them and kiss them goodnight, make sure all the presents are under the tree and that Santa didn't forget something, make their lunches for school, help with homework, take them to the doctor, take them to the park, encourage them to follow their dreams and believe in them that they can achieve them...

I don't have the luxury of another parent getting visitation with the kids every other weekend and on Wednesdays so I can have a break and some time to myself. I don't have someone else who will also lecture them about bad grades and making the right decisions in life. There is no one who might be able to take the day off work when they're sick because I don't have any more sick days left to take. I don't have anyone else who will show up to support them at soccer games, or pick them up from school if I'm running late, or who will be a confidant to them when they are mad at me but still need someone to talk to. I don't have a co-pilot in this thing.

I realize that divorced people don't *always* have that either, but the vast majority of them do. They both get to have a role in their child's life and participate in parenting. They have the option of deciding to be a part of the child's life- they make the choice about how involved they are going to be. We didn't get that option and it pisses me off.

I don't want to be the only parent...

Tue Mar 1, 2011 | 08:51 PM |
Ignorance is bliss...

"The most merciful thing in the world, I think, is the inability of the human mind to correlate all its contents. We live on a placid island of ignorance in the midst of black seas of infinity, and it was not meant that we should voyage far."
– H.P. Lovecraft, The Call of Cthulhu

I'm tired of trying to figure out the answer to the only real question I have: Why?

I am not meant to know the answer I suppose, or maybe there isn't one. It is hard for me to fathom not being able to find an answer...if I just look hard enough and long enough, surely the reason will be revealed, right? Is it a riddle I'm too dense to figure out? Is it so simple it's staring me in the face and I just can't see it?

I think I'm most terrified of not having the answer not for myself, but for these two innocent little girls who will without a doubt ask me this very question one day, to which I won't have an answer.

"Why did he have to die, Mommy?"
Perhaps I should be content with my ignorance and not voyage far...

Wed Mar 2, 2011 | 08:32 AM |
Perfection

People close to me think I'm a perfectionist. I used to think that too, but what I've realized is that I'm just afraid of not living up to the expectations of others. It's not an intrinsically driven thing in me that wants things to be "perfect" or "just so". It's that I don't want to disappoint anyone. Once you do something well once, then people come to expect that from you again. You've set the bar, so how do you then dip below it?

My issue is I just can't let people down, I must rise to the expectations of others...so I am driven to get good grades, to succeed, to have a nice house, to look put together and stay trim, to be good at my career, to be a good mom, to be financially savvy, to be a good listener, blah, blah, blah. All in an effort to make those who matter to me proud. I want to achieve so that I may appear "good enough" in the eyes of others...this probably definitely goes back to my own insecurities and issues with self-worth. I don't want to be a failure.

Andie's opinion was of course the most important one. I wanted him to be proud of me on every level. Now that he's gone I find myself not caring *so* much. Not worrying as much about whether or not I'm measuring up to the invisible bar I've set for myself because the judge is no longer around to give me a pass or fail. I'm beginning to be okay with things just being "good enough".

Andie thought I was perfect...he told me so a thousand times. In fact there was rarely a day that passed in which he did not give me some loving compliment that built me up and sustained me; that reassured me that I was actually "good enough". Yep, the majority of the time we were one of those couples that would make you gag if you knew how in love we were. We hid it pretty well in public, but in the privacy of our own home we were sickeningly in love and into each other.

He was always telling me I was beautiful, sexy, smart, a great wife, a great mom, I made a good dinner that night, he appreciated me and all the things I took care of around the house, I was the love of his life, I made him laugh, I was his whole world, I was awesome cause I got his favorite snack at the store, I was cool cause I never told him he couldn't go hunting or fishing, or any number of other things he loved about me. I was just *perfect*. I used to tell him that I hated when he told me I was perfect because it's not true and it set me up for failure; as there is no way I could ever live up to being perfect and I didn't want him to put me on that kind of pedestal. Being perfect is simply unrealistic and too much pressure. And he would always say, "Well, you're perfect *to me*." I remember arguing with him one day about not being perfect and I asked him if there was anything about me that irritated him. Nope, not a thing. There has to be *at least one thing* I do that you don't like, or wish I would change, or that you don't think is perfect. He thought for a moment and came up with 2 things.

1. I can't sing. (A very valid and indisputable accusation)
2. I never replaced the empty toilet paper roll; I just stacked a new roll on top of the empty roll.

Honestly, the only thing he ever complained about in our entire marriage is that I never put a new roll of toilet paper back on the holder...and he also didn't like the way I loaded the dishwasher. But those are honestly the only two things I remember him ever even commenting about. (I'm sure there were more things he didn't like, he was just too sweet to tell me). I think I subconsciously wouldn't put the toilet paper back on the roll just so that there would be something "imperfect" about me. To prove that he would love me anyway, even if there were imperfections.

Ironically, now I find myself replacing the empty toilet paper roll. Yes, ridiculously I do it now that he's gone. As if that will honor him in some absurd way. Oh, wouldn't he be so proud to be honored with a fresh roll of toilet paper on the holder!
And aren't I just the perfect little wife *now*... (cue eye rolling)

Sun Mar 6, 2011 | 01:35 PM |
I'll be alright...

I cleaned out Andie's sock and underwear drawer today. I threw all of it away except for a few pairs of his running socks that I kept for me to wear. The rest went into the trash. No sentimental value in underwear and socks so it wasn't too emotionally charged to get rid of it. I am now using that drawer to store the flags from his funeral, notes and pictures, memorabilia, and odds and ends that were his. I also cleaned out the armoire that I will be getting rid of in a couple of weeks. One of the drawers was mine and one was Andie's. Mine had almost every card and love note he had ever given me. I chose to pile them up and put them in a different drawer in my dresser without looking through them. I didn't have the emotional energy for that today.

Andie's drawer had his shoe polish stuff, several gun holsters, a magazine of bullets for his gun, a badge holder, random little things a man needs now and then. I kept most of it and tossed a few old receipts and things that were of no use. I thought I had emptied the whole drawer and was about to put it back in the armoire when I noticed something small in the back corner. It was a black elastic band. It took me a minute to figure out what it was. It was the black band that officers put around their badges when another officer has died to show respect for their fallen comrade. The kind that every officer that attended his funeral was wearing on their own badges that day. Ironic...he won't be needing that anymore. I almost threw it away but at the last second decided to keep it with his other police duty stuff.

It only took me about 30 minutes to go through all of this stuff. It was a small way to ease myself into what it will be like when I actually have to clean out his closet. Not that that will be anytime soon. Going through it all wasn't as hard as I thought it was going to be. Just had to give myself a little "push" to do it.

Guess I'm gonna be alright again after all...

Tue Mar 8, 2011 | 08:43 PM |
Existing

"Every life has dark tracts and long stretches of somber tint, and no representation is true to fact which dips its pencil only

in light, and flings no shadows on the canvas." – Alexander MacLaren

I find myself back in that place of a placid existence. The emotions dull and inaccessible, and for the most part even keeled. I do not cry on my drive to work anymore. I do not cry in the shower anymore. I have not had a night of deep sobs that are so loud I close myself in the bathroom so as not to wake the girls in quite a while. I do not cry so intensely that it makes my knees buckle anymore. I do not get angry when I have to take out the trash anymore. I do not pretend to believe he's coming home anymore.

I wonder what is wrong with me. Why do I not hurt more? Why am I not still an emotional wreck? Why do I only have 3 really rough days a month that happen to coincide with my period leading me to believe that the emotions are hormonally driven rather than true heartfelt, from the gut, emotions.

I know there is no "right" way to grieve, but if there's a wrong way I'm doing it. I begin to cry as I write this...the first good cry in a while because the thought that comes to mind when I see all of this in black and white is that it seems as if he doesn't matter to me anymore if I don't cry, and that is the furthest thing from the truth. I don't want people to think that I am better or healed or okay just because they don't see me being emotional. I am afraid that people will think I have forgotten him or gotten over the pain, and that will in turn give them permission to do the same.

Some would call this lack of emotional volatility progress or healing. I just call it existing. I don't know what else to do, really. I have come to terms with the fact that I cannot change this. He's not coming back and I have an entire lifetime that must be lived without him.

So I
Just. Keep. Existing.

Sun Mar 13, 2011 | 08:00 PM |

Enough already!

I don't even really know where to begin this post. I guess I could begin by saying that I'm exhausted, sick, overwhelmed, and have been pushed to the brink of breaking. If one more thing goes wrong in my life, I will truly lose it.

Essentially, I have spent the past 5 days in the hospital with Allie. Two weeks ago Allie and Addie both had fevers and a virus for several days. Addie bounced back but Allie never really seemed to get back up to full speed. She wasn't running a fever anymore, but she was irritable, cranky, and lethargic. I just kept thinking she would surely get over it soon.

Last Wednesday I came home from work and the nanny said Allie had been very tired and listless all day. She did not have a fever or any other symptoms of illness, but she was definitely not herself. She took a morning *and* afternoon nap (hasn't done that in months), and cried if she wasn't being held. When I fed her dinner that evening she refused to eat and was acting tired *again*. I put her down at 6:00 (a very early bedtime) and she fell right to sleep. I was very worried because it wasn't like her to be so lethargic and out of it. I was checking on her every 5-10 minutes to make sure she was breathing because I had a gut feeling that something was very wrong.

At 7:00 I woke her up to change her diaper and she was in better spirits. We were all sitting on the couch reading books and she was interacting well with Addie. All of a sudden she started moaning and writhing to get away from me. The next thing I knew, her body went limp, her eyes glazed over, and her lips turned blue; she was unresponsive to me calling her name. Within a second she was back responsive and moaning, but then it happened again. And again. I had a vivid flashback of the night Andie died, as this is how he looked when I rolled him over in bed that night. I panicked and called 911 fearing that she was having some sort of seizure. By the time EMS arrived she was back to normal. Her blood pressure and oxygen saturation were normal and she had no fever. They said she must've had a febrile seizure. I didn't believe them because she hadn't had a fever all day, but they insisted this was probably what it was.

I immediately took her to an ER to be evaluated. While we were waiting for test results to come back she started having episodes of clamminess and was passing gas that was strong enough to be smelled across the room. I thought maybe she was starting to get intussusception again (something we had a scare with back in August). The ER doctor said her head CT was normal, all her blood work was normal except that she was mildly anemic, and he did not feel she was having intussusception because she was not screaming and in extreme pain- a classic symptom of intussusception. He said to follow up with her pediatrician the next morning. We got home around midnight and until 2:30 Allie could not get comfortable. She writhed around and changed positions about every 10 seconds. Something she had done the first time she had intussusception...I had a gut feeling again that this was going on, but no verifiable symptoms to prove it. (It's usually diagnosed with a bloody stool, and crying bouts of extreme pain- which she had not had).

The next morning while waiting for the pediatrician's office to open so I could call them, she had a huge bloody stool. We rushed her to the ER at a children's hospital in San Antonio where it was such an emergency situation that they made us bypass triage, and got us set up immediately for ultrasounds to confirm the diagnosis. The ultrasound showed what looked like an atypical presentation of intussusception. Being that it was atypical and looked more swollen than a regular intussusception they said she must have emergency surgery to correct the situation; the usual protocol was an air enema but would be too dangerous in this situation and could risk perforating her bowel. Thursday afternoon she underwent surgery and did remarkably well. The surgeon found that she did not actually have intussusception, but instead had something called Meckel's Diverticulum. He resected that portion of her bowel and she should have no further complications. Turns out that what happened on Wednesday night wasn't a seizure, but was the result of her blood pressure dropping suddenly when she started to bleed internally.

She has been such a tough girl through all of this. She has had a great disposition and is healing up very quickly. Today she was able to start a liquid diet and if all goes as planned she will be discharged home tomorrow. We will be so excited to have her home!

Unfortunately, in all of this I have developed the worst chest cold I remember having in the past 10 years. I'm positive it is from all the stress. Sleeping in the hospital with her and traveling back and forth to spend time with Addie has been demanding physically and emotionally.

I am so very grateful to all my wonderful friends and family who have stepped up and provided immense support over the past five days. And to my boss who once again has been very understanding about my need to miss work.

I have so many emotions flooding around my head in regards to all of this. I was so terrified in the beginning and having bouts of PTSD. Thankfully, I am feeling relieved that she is okay, and grateful for good medical care. I feel like there is a dark cloud of bad luck looming over my head- I mean, how much more can one person take? But, then I am shown the love and support of all those around me when I am in need. I feel guilty that I am always having to call on someone or rely on others...it seems it's time for me to be paying back those in need, not still be the one who is always needy. I am frustrated that I had to go through all of this without my husband to support me. I am sad that I can't be with both of my kids at the same time. I am overwhelmed with being pulled in too many directions at once. I'm irritated that I was just getting back on my feet and independent again, and something happens that leaves me struggling to keep my head above water and relying on others to save me. I'm scared that people will get tired of always having to help me out and will just stop associating with me because my situation is too high maintenance, and there is "always something"...

I am exhausted.
I am tapped out.
I am at my breaking point.
I've been pushed too far.

I can't take one more thing...

Fri Mar 18, 2011 | 08:56 PM |
Re-birth

9 months today and my thoughts are scattered, but I keep coming back to the notion that it takes 9 months to grow a life. 9 months to nurture a baby in your womb. 9 months to create a living being and bring them into the world. Yet it takes only a second, just *one* moment, for a life to end.

I am bitter about that-there should have been a little more time. Sudden, unexpected death is so wrenching, ripping, aching, and mind-blowing. Similar to giving birth though there is no reward at the end of death. No gift in the end that is so great that it makes you forget all the pain you went through to get there, and be willing to do it all again for a just a little taste of the joy it brought.

No, in death you are left with nothing but the reverberating pain that echoes off itself. Continually bouncing back at you. Never knowing which angle it's coming from. Never really going away and always right below the surface. The pain never becomes a memory with death as it does after childbirth- the pain is always felt even if dulled with time. The sting is still there.

Those left in the wake are forced to re-birth themselves; to make themselves new in light of all that has been forced upon them. I am rebuilding myself; out of necessity, not by choice. Little by little learning who I am again. I'm angry about this too because I don't want to do this. It's hard. It's a struggle. Growing pains I guess. Angry because this process will take much longer than 9 months. Much longer.

I took the girls to his grave today for the first time. I showed Addie his temporary marker on the ground and said, "This is Daddy." She immediately kissed her hand as if blowing him a kiss and then touched the stone. Allie copied her. I cried as both of them continued to blow him kisses. How do they know to kiss a stone they have never seen, that only abstractly represents a father they barely remember? This blows my mind and is incomprehensible to me. We brought balloons to the grave. They each kissed their balloons and then let them go so we could send kisses to Daddy in heaven. They loved watching those balloons float away and all I could think is how badly I wish we could float away too. Drift somehow to a place where we could see him. Meet again even for just a minute.

But when that minute ended would the pain well up again as bad as the first time he was ripped away from me? Would I start all over again in this... this ugliness?

That I could not bear. So the alternative is to keep moving forward. Keep growing. Keep pushing...

Thu Mar 24, 2011 | 03:28 PM
Longing for past tense...

I have been thinking about who I am now that I don't have Andie to be my sounding board and reflect back to me all the things he loved about me. I defined myself by what I was to him. I feel exposed and flawed now without his unconditional love and support.

I find myself looking for validation in others, whether that be through constant venting, talking, and lamenting with my girl friends and colleagues (or anyone who will listen), or even harmless flirtatious banter with men whom I actually have *no* interest in. I feel like I've been thrown back to middle school where the desperation to "fit in" was all consuming. Just wanting to believe I am fun, smart, interesting, pretty, exciting, worthwhile...then I feel reproach for myself because I used to be really confident. I used to just care about the opinion of one person outside of myself. I don't like this desperate, clingy feeling. What happened to the put together girl I was? I want her back.

I don't want to feel the need to check my e-mail multiple times a day on the off chance that someone has something to share with me. I don't want to be disappointed when my mom has to go home after being with me for three days straight because I don't want to spend my evenings alone. I don't want the quiet loneliness to be so loud that it's actually deafening, so I find some noise, *any noise*, to fill it. I don't want to always be driven to constant distraction so I don't have to be alone with myself. I don't want to suddenly be hypersensitive about how I look in the hopes that if I at least *look* put together, then people will believe I'm put together. I don't even like admitting all of this is rattling around in my head because it all seems so pathetic.
I want to be okay with me again.

I want to be secure and confident, and not just put up a good front about it.

I want to be the girl that everyone thinks I am.

I want to be the girl I was... in the life I had.

Fri Mar 25, 2011 | 08:30 AM |
Tears...

"There is a sacredness in tears. They are not the mark of weakness, but of power. They speak more eloquently than ten thousand tongues. They are messengers of overwhelming grief...and unspeakable love." – Washington Irving

This morning the tears come as I'm getting ready for work. I was a little surprised by them because I hardly ever cry in the morning anymore. I realized I was having flashbacks of the night Andie died and reliving those awful moments at the hospital after he had been pronounced dead. I remember going outside to get some air and thinking, "My husband is dead. I have to call people. How is this real? *My* husband. Is *dead.*" I remember wanting to go back inside and demand that the doctors do some miraculous procedure that would save him. Cut him open and massage his heart by hand if they had to, anything that would offer one last chance at life. Then I remember having the thought that this sort of thing only happens on TV...rarely in real life.

I had worked through the flashbacks. Allowing myself to relive them in an effort to desensitize myself and process them. The only way to heal through them according to my grief counselor. I had gotten to the point where I could think about that night and not break down. *But*, after going through another traumatic event with Allie, seeing her become unresponsive and her lips turn blue, the flashbacks are back. My counselor warned me this would happen earlier this week when I saw her. "Be prepared," she had said. Traumatic memories are the strongest kind. They trigger other traumatic memories because they activate the same part of the brain, bypassing all the normal routes of memory consolidation. It's like a switch is flipped and there is nothing you can do about it. Except...live it again and again until it doesn't hurt so badly.

I also realize this morning that I have not had any dreams about Andie in a while. Nor have I felt his presence with me as I so often did in the early days. It leaves me feeling abandoned and angry. Again...just as I did on the night he died. Perhaps this is why I have been clinging desperately to any sort of connection with others lately. It's irrational to feel abandoned; I know he would have never chosen to leave us. I cry about this too this morning. Feeling so alone...and irrational.

Trying to appreciate the power of my tears...

To understand that while they *are* messengers of overwhelming grief, so too, do they represent *unspeakable* love...

Survivor

Yesterday I had to get my tire replaced. It had an industrial staple in the side and couldn't be patched. So I had to buy a whole new tire. This was of course something Andie *would've* handled.

The attendant at the tire store started asking me questions about the car and our previous service there. He looked up the account under my name but didn't find anything. He searched by my last name and remarked that there were a lot of "Simmons" in the system. "Well, if you have an Andie, that was my husband," I replied. Before I could catch myself I referred to him in the past tense. The attendant caught my slip. "Did you say *was*?" he said as he glances at the ring on my finger. *Crap.* I hate when I do this. I had been referring to him in the present tense to avoid this very conversation.

I tell him my husband passed away 9 months ago. He offers heartfelt condolences and seems shocked beyond belief. *So* shocked he remarks about how young I am and asks my age. "What are you, 25? 27?" I tell him I'm 30, my husband was only 34. He wants to know if he was in the military. No, he had a heart condition. I'm barely holding back tears at this point. Luckily, he changes the subject back to the car. He goes out to the car to check the mileage giving me a second to compose myself. When he comes back in he asks if I have kids. I think his knees almost buckled when I told him I have 19 month old twins. Again we go through the rounds of condolences and look of utter shock on his face. "You are one strong woman," he tells me. I chuckle at this thinking to myself that being a survivor doesn't necessarily make you strong. "I just do what I have to do," I reply. Holding back tears once again, because when I hear it all spoken out loud it's just *so* damn sad. And so unreal...

Yep, I just do what I have to do. Like take the car to the tire store to get a new tire. And tell people over and over that my husband is dead. And tell *myself* over and over that my husband is dead. And try to remember that when the car hits 55,000 miles I will need all new tires, and will need to rotate the one I bought yesterday to the front. And I keep surviving.

I just do what I have to do...
Cause he's not here to do it for me anymore.

Sat Apr 2, 2011 | 08:47 PM |
Passing through...

I traveled out of my comfort zone today. I drove two-lane back country roads to a small town in Texas with a population of less than 1000. It was the same route I drove countless days to and from work over 4 years ago. It was the same area that Andie once patrolled while on duty. I couldn't help but think that I was following the very path he did on many days. Wondering what he was thinking as he saw the very same things I saw today while he was just passing through...

A bucolic setting; most of the drive picturesque farmland and pastures. I passed some corn fields. Freshly baled hay. Horses and cows grazing. I drove past the house of the deputy who was recently reassigned Andie's unit number and thought about how time keeps moving and doesn't stop on account of the mourning. I flashed back to how sucker-punched I felt the day I found out that his number had been reassigned. Some other deputy would be checking on the radio as unit 146...he essentially no longer existed even as a number.

I drove past an old man driving a tractor down the road. He waved in a true friendly Texas fashion. I passed the truck stop where Andie used to get free coffee every morning that he was on duty. I again pass another old man driving a tractor down the road and marvel that some of the old ways of life still exist. The winding, curvy road takes me through a small town of less than 500. Most of the crossroads I pass are named after people, mostly of Polish decent. Those who settled this area centuries ago. Again, I am reminded that time keeps moving. None of those who settled the area and had roads named after them are still here. It feels like a whole other lifetime that I once traveled these roads on a daily basis. It *was* a different life for me then...one I seemed to just pass through.

I traveled this way today to pay respects to a former colleague who passed away earlier this week; another young husband and father taken too soon from his family. It was the first memorial service I have attended since my own husband's. I held myself together pretty well. My eyes welled up with tears when they played one of the same songs that was played at Andie's funeral, but my breath didn't catch in my throat until I talked to his wife. Until I had to look her in the eye.

In her eyes I saw the shock and devastation. I saw a woman who could not yet comprehend what her life was becoming. I saw what the rest of the world calls "strong" as she held herself together and greeted everyone. I know the truth behind that strength. I know she is merely surviving, existing, breathing. In her eyes I saw the searching...searching for reassurance that she is in a nightmare and none of this is real. Searching for comfort. Searching for answers.

In her eyes I saw me...

Tue Apr 5, 2011 | 09:16 AM |
Intangible...

The necklace with his ring on it is sitting on my bathroom counter amongst a pile of random jewelry that I haven't gotten around to putting back in its proper place in my jewelry box. I took it off 9 days ago. I thought I'd make it to a year at least before I decided I didn't need the weight of its security around my neck.

I took it off mainly because I got sunburned that weekend and it was irritating the back of my neck. I had intentions of putting it back on when my sunburned faded. But I didn't. And I'm okay with that.

At least I feel like I'm okay with it. I haven't missed it over the past 9 days. I've enjoyed being able to wear some of my other necklaces that have been patiently waiting their turn in my jewelry box.

But, ever the analytical one, I worry that I'm just deluding myself into thinking I'm more healed than I am. I worry that I'm not really working the grief these days, but just putting it on a shelf to deal with later. I'm afraid that I feel *too* okay about this. I worry that I should not be doing so well. I feel like I should be hurting more. I should be searching for joy, not already finding it. I should be hoping for peace, not experiencing it. I should be wracked with guilt about disconnecting from him, even if it's only in a symbolic way; not resigned to the quiet acceptance of it.

What I've realized is that holding onto the tangible doesn't make him any less intangible. Wearing his necklace with his ring on it, continuing to wear my wedding ring, keeping his clothes in the closet right where he left them…none of it means that he's not gone.

My biggest fear is that the more I heal, the more I fear I will forget him.

And that is what makes the pain return and the tears fall.

The thought of him being just a faded memory when all I want is for him to still be vivid, and real, and tangible.

Thu Apr 7, 2011 | 12:39 PM |
Thinking of you...

This time of year is hard-It was our favorite time of year. The weather is turning nice and we loved to be outdoors more. You loved to BBQ and take walks around the neighborhood. You liked sprucing up the yard...taking pride in how it looked. The wildflowers are blooming. The hill country becomes pretty again. The changing of the seasons reminds me that I am edging closer to the time last year when you died. I'm flooded with memories of things. It seems almost anything these days can make me think of you. Do you think of us too? Are you still here?

I wonder if I will always have you so fresh on my brain and readily accessible. So much reminds me of you.

I'll think of you when...
I eat ice cream
I smell the familiar aroma of a grill lighting up
I hear a fish jump at the lake
I see someone wearing the kind of fishing shirts you had taken to wearing, almost exclusively
I see a jeep

And I'll think of you when...
I drive down hill country roads always scanning to look for deer or other wildlife like you used to do
I see a center console fishing boat- just the kind you always admired.
I pass a Dairy Queen that has their blizzard of the month posted on the marquee
I see a police car crest a hill on the horizon in oncoming traffic. It still makes my heart stop for a split second thinking it could be you...
I sit on the dock at the lake house soaking up the sun, feeling your presence
I hear the familiar rumble of a loud truck down the street
I eat at Herbert's Taco Hut or make spaghetti- your favorite dish of mine

I replace the empty toilet paper roll
I load the dishwasher...trying my hardest to do it as you taught
me. To pack in as much as possible

And I'll think of you when...
Summer rolls around- our favorite time of year.
Or when someone mentions Texas Hold 'em, and I remember
the time we went to Port Aransas to gamble on the boat there
and I forgot my ID and we had to drive all the way back to where
we were staying to get it because they wouldn't let me on the
boat without it. You were so irritated with me and teased me
about it ever since.
And when someone mentions the border or Del Rio. We had a
horrible trip there but laughed about it for years afterward.
Whenever I see a weimaraner. I gave you a weim puppy for our
first anniversary. We took him to Kerrville for a weekend
getaway (against your wishes and better judgment) and had to
come home in the middle of the night when he threw up on us in
the bed. We laughed about that one for years too.
When I'm tired and being an only parent seems unbearable

And I'll especially think of you when...
I look at our children and hear them laugh and watch them grow
into beautiful women- the kind you'd be proud of
When I wake and realize your side of the bed is still empty
When I finally make a decision about whether or not to keep
pursuing *our* dreams, or start making some of my own
And when I have to make the hard decisions in life...and the
easy ones too

I will think of you when...
One day, I have found myself again

And I will think of you too, when the bluebonnets bloom...

Fri Apr 8, 2011 | 09:23 PM |
Believe...

"Truth is simply whatever you bring yourself to believe."
–Alice Childress

Not long after Andie died I read a couple books pertaining to signs that our loved ones give us from the other side. I was terrified of missing some sign or communication due to lack of knowledge about the subject. One of the most common ways that our loved ones communicate, according to both books I read, is through electrical currents. Often flickering lights, or burned out lights, or things turning on and off for no apparent reason.

Four months after Andie died I decided to have the kitchen backsplash tiled. It was something he and I had discussed many times but never did because he didn't want to spend the money. He thought it was frivolous. When the tile guy came to give me the bid and measure the backsplash we discussed why I was deciding to do it. I jokingly said that I was doing it because my husband never wanted me to and now he wasn't around anymore to tell me "no". That day, one of the recessed lights in the kitchen went out. We've never had any of the recessed lights go out in this house since we moved in. When it happened I joked that it was Andie's way of giving me a sign that he *still* disapproved of having the backsplash done. I replaced the bulb and didn't think anything of it again. A couple of weeks later the guys showed up to actually install the backsplash. That day another bulb blew out; a completely different one from the first one. And I started to really wonder if it was in fact a sign from Andie.

I have since had between 6-8 light bulbs go out in my kitchen in the last 6 months alone. The last two that burned out I never replaced because I got scared that I must have an electrical short and I didn't want to risk a fire. They've been burned out for several weeks now.

I had an electrician come to the house today to take a look. He checked the switches that turn the lights on. Both were perfectly fine. Then he went into the attic to make sure there wasn't a short, or a wiring problem. All looked good- so good that he complimented how great of a job the electrician that wired the house had done. I showed him the light bulbs I have been using to make sure I wasn't buying the wrong kind or wrong wattage. They were exactly what I needed according to him.

He said he had no reasonable explanation for why my lights would randomly be burning out. He said it was "strange" that it wasn't always the same light, and that it wasn't always burning out in the same way. For instance, sometimes they burn out after they've been on for a while, and other times when they've been off and you flip the switch they pop and go out. He said sometimes recessed lights go out when they overheat but then they come back on. He'd never heard of them popping and blowing like mine do, and he couldn't think of a reason that this would be happening. He said he'd talk with some other electricians that he knew to see if they had ever come across this problem, but it was nothing he could fix because there was nothing even wrong. Everything looked perfect.

"There's one more thing I want to tell you," he said before he left. "You're a really good mother. You're so attentive to your girls." I was almost brought to tears by the sincerity of the compliment, and by the fact that it was so out of context from the rest of our conversation. Especially since he had only been in my house and able to observe me with my kids for a couple of hours. I have to admit that for half a second I wondered if Andie was speaking to me through this man, perhaps sending me a message...

The fervor to see signs from Andie isn't as strong anymore.

I feel more content with the unknown than I did in the early days when answers and absolutes seemed necessary.

I still don't know what I believe about signs from the other side. I'm still trying to find my own truth in that.

But I have to admit that after what happened today, my interest is piqued...

Sun Apr 10, 2011 | 07:39 PM |
Finding joy...

"Today is the tomorrow you were worried about yesterday. Was it worth it?" – Siddhartha

I had a great weekend. On Saturday I took the girls to the lake for a little while and they got to swim and play in the water. It was joyous to soak up a couple hours of sunlight and bask in the glow of their smiles. Today my mom met me at the Home and Garden Show and then we decided to head over to a local BBQ joint to hear some live music that the local radio show was broadcasting. The girls were gloriously behaved all day. It was exactly the kind of weekend that Andie and I loved. The reason we chose to live in this quaint little town that always has some fun activity going on.

On the way home I was thinking to myself that this was the first time in a long time that I have felt like life really might be worth it after all. I felt like there might actually be things to look forward to. We walked in the door and mom flipped the switch to turn on the kitchen light. Another bulb blew. The first in many, many weeks. I smiled and cried a little thinking he must be with us enjoying the perfect weekend and just wanted to let us know he was here.

I actually cooked a real meal for dinner. Only the third or fourth time I've done it since Andie passed. It felt good to feel like a "real mom" who actually puts a home cooked meal on the table and eats with her kids. Usually I throw together kid food and then skip dinner for myself. Tonight I savored the tilapia and zucchini ("nini" as the kids call it). It was one of Andie's favorite dishes of mine.

After bath time the girls were giddy. They horse played and loved on each other for about 30 minutes straight- giggling the whole time. As any mother knows, there is no better sound than that of your children's laughter. I even got some spontaneous kisses out of them. Bonus!

All in all it was a wonderful weekend, one in which I found some joy.

Of course there was a huge piece missing, but for once I was able to not focus on that. I was able to focus on what was actually in front of me.

And for once I was able to not worry about tomorrow...

Wed Apr 13, 2011 | 08:53 PM |
Spirit...

I have a wooden sign in my living room that says:
"Spirit: Strength and courage aren't always measured in medals and victories. They are measured in the struggles they overcome. The strongest people aren't always the people who win, they are the people who don't give up when they lose."

We've got spirit yes we do, we've got spirit, how bout you?

I remember that grade school cheerleading chant so well...

We widows tend to shy away from the compliments we get about being strong. It feels undeserved to say we are strong when we are only doing what must be done to survive. We didn't choose to walk through the fire, we were forced to and we feel the burn. So we feel like a fraud to take on the "strong" label because it doesn't feel like we rightfully earned it. It was just given to us. But the truth is we *are* strong. And we should own it. Not everyone can suffer a devastating loss and continue to move through the world with grace and poise. Not everyone can lose everything that ever mattered and still choose to get up the next morning and keep going. Not everyone can continue to hold their head up while in the depths of deep despair. But *we* do. Not because it's something we wanted or chose, but because we have to. We choose *not* to give up when we lose.

And in the words of a current Sugarland song, "Sometimes you gotta lose til you win."

So maybe we shy away from being called strong. Perhaps we could wear the "spirit" label better. We are strong and we are courageous, *because* we have spirit.

My aunt gave me this sign and I love it.
Because it speaks to me about the unbroken spirit.
It speaks to me about getting back up when life has knocked you down.
Pushing back when life pushes you.
It speaks to me about bouncing back. Getting back on the proverbial horse.
It speaks to me of resilience.

And *that* is something I can own...

Mon Apr 18, 2011 | 08:06 PM |
Charades...

Ten months today and it still does not seem real to me. Many days I feel like he is on an extended trip and most definitely will return soon. I delude myself into thinking that this is all not really happening. It is only in small increments that my mind can process that he is never going to walk through the door again.

I dreaded this anniversary because the girls were only 10 months old when he died, and I feared that it would be hard to consider that half their lives he has not been with them. It is sad to think that from this day forward they will have had more time *without* him than with him. I am particularly sad for my girls today- more so than for me. I am hit with the gravity of how much they will miss. Have *already* missed. How little they knew of him. I had almost 10 years with him, they only 10 months. Months they will never remember. And no matter how much I tell them about him, they will never *truly* know him like I did.

I am extremely sad that in all likelihood they will one day think of another man as their father. I want them to have a father figure and I want them to have the emotional connection with a man they can love, trust, admire, and look up to. But I am not okay with the fact that it will not be with their father. The man who helped create them. Who loved them with every ounce of his being just because they were his. I am not ready to accept that another man could love them as much, and as well as their own father. And for that I feel angry that they are the ones getting cheated. How do you ever begin to accept second best for your children?

Every night as I take them to bed we stop at his picture and tell him goodnight, that we love him, and that we want him to visit us in our dreams so we can tell him about our day. I wonder when the day will come when they ask me why we talk to this picture. Who is this man that we have to say goodnight to?

For on that day, the charade will end and I just *might* actually believe that he's really gone...

Thu Apr 21, 2011 | 10:18 PM |
April...

Around this time 10 years ago Andie kissed me for the first time and we never were apart after that day. April 11, 2001. A day that will be etched in my mind for eternity. A moment that changed my entire future.

This time last year, in April, Andie and I had just closed on 2.5 acres of property in the hill country on which we were to build our dream house. We knew it would take us a couple of years to plan and save, but we had a plan. Signing those papers was a moment that we thought would change our entire future.

Strange how it takes just *one* moment to change your entire future.

Whether you plan for it or not...

{PART FOUR}

FOUND...

He will wipe away every tear from their eyes, and death shall be no more, neither shall there be mourning, nor crying, nor pain anymore, for the former things have passed away.
Revelation 21:4 ESV

Mon Apr 25, 2011 | 12:19 PM |
Beginning afresh...

"Be patient with everyone, but above all with yourself. I mean, do not be disturbed because of your imperfections, and always rise up bravely from a fall. I'm glad that you make daily a new beginning; there is no better means of progress in the spiritual life than to be continually beginning afresh." – Francis de Sales

I'm trying to remember to learn to be patient with myself. This process of grief is long, hard, and often paradoxical in the way it forces you to yearn for an old life while also learning to appreciate the new one you've been given. "To be continually beginning afresh"...

Yesterday was a particularly hard and emotional day for me. I had no idea I was going to get blindsided by it. One of the songs we sang in church was one that we played at Andie's funeral. Then we went to his parents' house for lunch and for the kids to do an Easter egg hunt. All I could think about was this day last year when the girls were not even walking yet, and Andie and I talked about how fun it would be this year to see them actually hunt for eggs. It was like a movie continually being replayed over and over in my mind, of how this day was just a short year ago.

The "firsts" of my birthday, the girls' birthday, and our wedding anniversary came so soon after he died that I was still in a complete fog of shock and disbelief. I was still completely numb, so they didn't hurt. For Christmas this year we went out of town-something completely out of the ordinary so I didn't have to be at home doing the same old routine and traditions. So Easter was the first holiday that was kind of the same ol' thing. It was the first holiday that I've come across so far that felt routine and familiar. And in the routine and familiar, the pain seeps in because the void of the person missing is so apparent.

And while all of this hurts deeply, and makes me question if I've made any progress at all rather than just spiraling back around to the same issues, I'm still finding things to be joyful in. I'm still learning to appreciate new experiences, new friends, and a new way of life for myself. I'm finally getting to the point where I can accept, albeit in small doses, that happy experiences don't mean I love him any less. I can hurt and ache for him, and still hold love and fulfillment in my heart- it's not all or nothing. It doesn't mean that if I have one, I can't have the other.

It just means that healing is taking root. Hope is on the horizon. It means that I make daily a new beginning.
Each day I begin afresh.
Each day I rise up bravely from the fall...

Tue Apr 26, 2011 | 02:40 PM |
Finding meaning...

"Grief turns out to be a place none of us know until we reach it. We anticipate (we know) that someone close to us could die, but we do not look beyond the few days or weeks that immediately follow such an imagined death. We misconstrue the nature of even those few days or weeks. We might expect if the death is sudden to feel shock. We do not expect this shock to be obliterative, dislocating to both body and mind. We might expect that we will be prostrate, inconsolable, crazy with loss. We do not expect to be literally crazy, cool customers who believe that their husband is about to return and need his shoes. In the version of grief we imagine, the model will be "healing". A certain forward movement will prevail. The worst days will be the earliest days. We imagine that the moment to most severely test us will be the funeral, after which the hypothetical healing will take place. When we anticipate the funeral we wonder about failing to "get through it," rise to the occasion, exhibit the "strength" that invariably gets mentioned as the correct response to death. We anticipate needing to steel ourselves for the moment: will I be able even to get dressed that day? We have no way of knowing that this will not be the issue. We have no way of knowing that the funeral itself will be

anodyne, a kind of narcotic regression in which we are wrapped in the care of others and the gravity and meaning of the occasion. Nor can we know ahead of the fact (and here lies the heart of the difference between grief as we imagine it and grief as it is) the unending absence that follows, the void, the very opposite of meaning, the relentless succession of moments during which we will confront the experience of meaninglessness itself." - Joan Didion in The Year of Magical Thinking

There is a dissonance between grief as we imagine it and grief as it is. They are rarely one in the same, never really rising to the expectation of the other.

We search for meaning in all of it, often finding no satisfactory answer. Eventually relegating ourselves to the fact that we are not meant to know the answers, or it is futile to continue the relentless search. Giving up on finding meaning.

But sometimes, just sometimes you find meaning where you thought there was none to find.

What you think is going to knock you on your ass and throw you for a loop is sometimes exactly what you needed to PUSH forward...to confront that which you so feared.

And in the quest to find your purpose, you give your life new meaning.

Fri Apr 29, 2011 | 08:27 PM |
A Big Step...

"I am not discouraged, because every wrong attempt discarded is another step forward." – Thomas Edison

I have taken a huge step in this grief process.
I have taken off my wedding ring.

I feel the need to keep pushing myself onward through this and I can't co-exist in two worlds. One in which I am still betrothed to my husband, and one in which I will allow new relationships and new beginnings into my life. I cannot continue to be committed to someone who is not here. "Til death do us part"...I said those very vows and I thought that I meant them. Turns out I meant "Til death do us part, plus 10 months *just* to be sure".

So in an effort to keep moving and keep growing, to get out of the stagnation of grief, I have done something that tells the world that I am no longer married. I feel at ease and at peace with the decision. Something I could not even fathom just weeks ago.

It has taken me a long time to accept this for myself. I have taken a few steps forward and many steps back in this process. I know my steps will continue to falter along the way.

But I'm ready to embrace the new life set before me.

The life I must now cultivate and create based on *my* needs.

And I simply cannot do that if I stay married to a dead man.

Mon May 9, 2011 | 02:44 PM |
Ugly side

Looking back at some recent interactions I have had with those close to me I realize now how emotionally guarded I must have been my whole life. I didn't really understand how much I have kept people at a distance. And *continue* to keep others at a distance...until now. Now I see me for what I am: vulnerable, terrified of getting hurt, afraid to show weakness.

It is hard for me to accept that sometimes "good things" just happen...I've always felt like the kind of person who draws in the "bad things happen to good people" vibe from the universe so I always have my guard up. I'm in a constant state of hyperawareness, overanalyzing, planning my escape route. Waiting for the other proverbial shoe to drop, and never wanting someone else to get the best of me. It takes me a long time to trust someone and even those who are in my closest inner circle rarely get a glimpse of how I truly feel. I'm a born skeptic, constantly thinking about the "what ifs". I find myself pushing the limits to see how far I can go, sure that when I cross the limit and someone finally gives up on me, I can stand back and place the blame on them for not being able to take all that I dish out. Not always giving due credit for what they *did* do and how long they did endure.

Ridiculously immature of me. I see now the ugly side of me. The martyr, the "woe is me", the "can't I catch a break" whiny side. I wonder how difficult Andie must have found it to be in this constant sparring match of wits with me. Always trying to stay one step ahead and continually reassure me. Sometimes feeling as though he could never win...in truth, cause he couldn't. I never let him. I see now that when I thought he was giving up on me, he was really just refusing to engage in a losing battle. Knowing I'd always come around somehow. I want to tell him how sorry I am. That I didn't realize how difficult I was being. That if he were still here I'd start letting him win every now and then. Recently, I have begun to embrace the idea of sharing my honest feelings and have been surprised by how freeing it is to allow someone to see through you. To the *real* you. And I like it.

The grief process is funny; it's not always about the grief. More often it turns out to be about you and your underlying issues. It continually challenges us to reevaluate who we are and face things we were never forced to face before, and in doing so we have a new perspective on who we *once* were. We see ourselves through a vastly different lens. It's not always fun, and it's definitely not always pretty.

I realize now how unfair it is to keep people at a distance. I want to let them in.

I want to be able to share myself on a genuine level.
I just have to start letting go of the fear...

Wed May 11, 2011 | 03:36 PM |
Connection...

In the beginning there is an obsession with the one who has died. A desperation for the thread to not unravel, to hold all that you had as couple together for as long as possible by trying to keep every memory you have in immediate awareness. Striving to stay connected by any means possible. Eventually some acceptance settles in that no matter how hard you try, there is no way to keep them alive through memories alone. The constant drive to stay connected tapers off; the fire within subdues and the rumination lies dormant.

After a while there is a stirring inside. Something sparks a curiosity. A yearning for new connection.

Real.
Human.
Connection.

A desire to be fulfilled by another. To be appreciated, understood, comforted, and admired.

There is a longing to be touched. To be whispered to. To develop the subtle give and take that comes when two people develop a unique bond and share in the human experience together.

Once you've experienced fulfilling love the desperation to have it again can be intense. At times, the desire to interact with another on a level that is unique to only the two of you can be powerful and overtaking. I find myself watching other couples in public. Jealous of the nuance between them that only *they* truly understand. A certain look, a tilt of the head, a hand placed on the shoulder just so.

When you know what you're missing, you suddenly have a new appreciation for it and seek to find it again. Perhaps that is why they say that widows who were in fulfilling and happy marriages tend to remarry sooner...because they crave that kind of closeness.

Eventually the rumination returns, but with a new focus when you begin to see that you might find another worthy of your attention, and they in return may also find you worthy.

When it comes within striking distance you seize it for fear it will get away.
For fear that you might miss your one shot to be truly happy again.
And the connection becomes the new obsession...

Fri May 13, 2011 | 12:28 PM |
Peace...

I saw this quote on another widow blog and it spoke to me. I've been coming back to it for days, letting it seep into my consciousness. Thought I'd let you all know what has been occupying my thoughts...

Desiderata by Max Ehrmann

"Go placidly amid the noise and the haste, and remember what peace there may be in silence. As far as possible, without surrender, be on good terms with all persons. Speak your truth quietly and clearly; and listen to others, even to the dull and the ignorant; they too have their story. Avoid loud and aggressive persons; they are vexatious to the spirit. If you compare yourself with others, you may become vain or bitter, for always there will be greater and lesser persons than yourself. Enjoy your achievements as well as your plans. Keep interested in your own career, however humble; it is a real possession in the changing fortunes of time. Exercise caution in your

business affairs, for the world is full of trickery. But let this not blind you to what virtue there is; many persons strive for high ideals, and everywhere life is full of heroism. Be yourself. Especially do not feign affection. Neither be cynical about love, for in the face of all aridity and disenchantment, it is as perennial as the grass. Take kindly the counsel of the years, gracefully surrendering the things of youth. Nurture strength of spirit to shield you in sudden misfortune. But do not distress yourself with dark imaginings. Many fears are born of fatigue and loneliness. Beyond a wholesome discipline, be gentle with yourself. You are a child of the universe no less than the trees and the stars; you have a right to be here. And whether or not it is clear to you, no doubt the universe is unfolding as it should. Therefore be at peace with God, whatever you conceive Him to be. And whatever your labors and aspirations, in the noisy confusion of life, keep peace in your soul. With all its sham, drudgery, and broken dreams, it is still a beautiful world. Be cheerful. Strive to be happy.”

This line especially speaks to me:

"And whether or not it is clear to you, no doubt the universe is unfolding as it should. Therefore be at peace with God, whatever you conceive Him to be."

I am finding peace...
finally.

Wed May 18, 2011 | 03:00 PM |
11...

11 months today. So close to a full year. What's the difference really, between now and one more month? No difference in the grand scheme of things. It has all gone by so fast. I think about a conversation I had with a friend when the girls were younger. We were talking about how you report your children's age in weeks for a while, then in months. There is no clear transition as

to when to switch over. Are they 24 weeks old, or 6 months? I feel the same about this...when do I stop counting the months and start counting years. At 13 months will I say my husband passed a year ago or will I continue to mark the months in time? This morning as I am getting ready for work I think about what jewelry I want to wear. I have a little pile of jewelry that holds special meaning on my counter. I choose the necklace with my Push and 10-4 charms. I put my wedding ring on my right hand as many widows do. It's the first time I've put it back on in any capacity since I took it off a few weeks ago. The weight of it feels good, like it's meant to be there. I put my pink gold anniversary bands that he bought me in honor of the twins on my left hand. I have lost so much weight that I must wear them on my middle finger now. Shoving them over the knuckle I broke in middle school that healed crooked. I feel like this is a metaphor for my life: shoving past things to make myself fit. To try to get back to normal.

I go to put on my socks and realize the ones I pull out are his. They are slightly too big for my slender feet but I wear them anyway. Last night I wore one of his "Sheriff" t-shirts to bed.

I guess subconsciously I'm trying to stay connected through tangible symbols, but feel more and more like I'm losing grip on it. The always tenuous and delicate connection to him feels like it is slowly fading.

I visit his grave before work. The tears flow easily this morning as I listen to some of the music from his funeral and several other songs that remind me of him. Like a teenager who self-mutilates just to feel something rather than feeling numb, I choose to listen to this music to get to that deep place of emotion I rarely allow myself to visit. It is cathartic to release the tears and I feel better.

As I drive to work I recall a conversation I had with my ob/gyn yesterday. It was the first time she has seen me since my follow up after the girls were born. I talked on the phone with her right after Andie died but hadn't seen her until now. She wants to know how I'm doing- how I'm *really* doing. She commends me on how well put together I seem. She comments that I have "strong faith" after I tell her I just do what I have to do to keep going on most days. She says I'm doing a great job to be raising the girls alone. All I can think is how great I've gotten at putting up a good facade most of the time. She asks to see pictures of the girls and is stunned by how much they look like him. "I can just see him sitting right there in that chair," she says pointing to where he sat during my exams. "As if it were just yesterday," are the unsaid words hanging in the air. We give each other a knowing glance and she hugs me. I wonder how long I will run in to people who don't know or I haven't seen since his death and I have to have the awkward conversations.

I realize that though the connection feels like it is slipping he is still here. Not in the way we all want, but in the only way he can be. In our memories, in the faces of our children, and in our hearts.

"You're still here" by Faith Hill

Thought I saw you today
You were standing in the sun then you turned away
And I know it couldn't be
But my heart believed
Oh it seems like there's something everyday
How could you be so far away?
When you're still here
When I need you you're not hard to find
You're still here
I can see you in my baby's eyes
And I laugh and cry
You're still here
I had a dream last night
That you came to me on silver wings
And I flew away with you on a painted sky
And I woke up wondering what was real
Is what you see and touch or what you feel
'Cause you're still here

Oh you're everywhere we've ever been
You're still here
I heard you in a strangers laugh
And I hung around to hear him laugh again
Just once again
Thought I saw you today
You were standing in the sun then you turned away

Sun May 22, 2011 | 03:24 PM |

Finding our way...

"Out of every crisis comes the chance to be reborn, to reconceive ourselves as individuals, to choose the kind of change that will help us grow and fulfill ourselves more completely."– Nena O'Neill

I attended a new church today with the girls. Just the three of us. Just our little family. Starting something new on our own-making a new way of life for ourselves. I am in a phase of rebirthing who I am and who our family will be without Andie in it. It's a necessary part of the healing process for me to find my own way again...to choose the kind of change that will help me grow into who I want to be. Only when I find my own way, can I successfully lead the girls and be the strong parent they deserve.

Religion was always a minor point of contention with Andie and me. Me being raised Methodist, and him being raised Church of Christ, we didn't always see things the same way. Before we got married we talked about what religion we'd like to practice and how we'd like to raise our kids one day, but the reality of how we led our lives was far different from the hypothetical conversations we had. As is often the case with these kind of issues.

We said we would allow both religions to be a part of our lives as neither one of us wanted to completely give up who we were in that sense. We would alternate which church we attended, or just find a new one that we both felt comfortable in.

But the reality was that we always went to his church. Only when I really pushed did he agree to visit a Methodist church a time or two. It became something that I acquiesced on just to keep the peace. We didn't go to church often mainly because he was usually working, but also because it wasn't hugely important to him. And since I didn't have a strong connection with his religion I didn't push the issue. We went when we went. It wasn't something either one of us felt convicted to do because we hadn't established a strong bond with the church as a couple.

But through this process my yearning for a deeper spiritual understanding has increased. I have been longing to reestablish that part of my life. To rebuild myself, and to rebuild my relationship with God.

So I tried something new today in the hopes that I just might fulfill myself more completely. In the hopes that maybe I can navigate my way out of this grief and lead us as a family into a new way of life we can call our own.

Mon May 23, 2011 | 09:29 AM |
New...

"Were it possible for us to see further than our knowledge reaches, and yet a little way beyond the outworks of our divining, perhaps we would endure our sadnesses with greater confidence than our joys. For they are the moments when something new has entered into us, something unknown; our feelings grow mute in shy perplexity, everything in us withdraws, a stillness comes, and the new, which no one knows, stands in the midst of it and is silent." – Maria Rainer Rilke

So I was watching Oprah the other day and they showed a clip from an old show when Dr. Phil used to be on as a guest. He was talking with a woman who was stuck in her grief, 10 years after losing her daughter. She had not been able to move on and let go of the pain and anger. He said something to her that struck a chord with me.

He asked her if her daughter would feel betrayed in some way by her mother moving on and leading a happy life. The lady of course replied that her daughter would not feel betrayed by her moving on, but rather would actually be mad at her mother for continuing to be miserable every day. Her daughter wouldn't want that kind of life for her.

Dr. Phil replied, "Maybe the betrayal is focusing on the day of her death and not on the event of her life."

This hit close to home for me. I find myself continuing to struggle with the idea of moving forward, finding joy, and living again rather than merely existing. Sometimes I feel like it is a betrayal to not still be debilitated with grief. But at the same time, I'm *really* tired of being emotionally drained, and want to have the same optimism about life that I used to carry with me before I became a widow.

Hearing Dr. Phil reframe it in this way made me realize that I can celebrate the life he had and the life we had together, without focusing on his death, which was really only *one* day in the grand scheme of his life. He is so much more than his death. He truly would not want me to be miserable every day. He would want me to feel fulfilled, and excited about life and my future. He would celebrate how far I've come, and he would encourage me to continue to carve out a new life for myself.

Many days I still feel caught between two worlds. The life I had, and the new life I must now create. Going through this process is like being stripped to the core and rebuilding from scratch. Relearning what you value, how you view things, and who you want to be.

As the quote above says, "...a stillness comes, and the new, which no one knows, stands in the midst of it and is silent."

A stillness, a sense of peace eventually comes and you realize that it is okay to be new again. To start over.

The newness stands silent, waiting patiently, until you are ready to accept that it is there, then it welcomes you with open arms and allows you to become whatever it is that you want to be...

Fri May 27, 2011 | 12:41 PM |
Contingency plan...

This morning I went to a meeting with the committee planning the 5k in honor of Andie. It feels good to be doing something to honor and celebrate his life. I am pleased that I have chosen this as a way to mark the one year anniversary of his death, and I hope that it can be a peaceful day for those who loved him to come together in friendship and have a good time.

After that I had to go to another meeting. A meeting that will essentially memorialize him and permanently mark the end of his life. I went to the cemetery office today to finalize the plans for his grave stone. I picked out the design very early after he died. I was still in a complete haze of disorientation then, so I ask her to show me what I picked because I honestly don't remember...I was pleased to find that even in the shock of grief I still had good taste. Though expensive taste I am reminded, when I have to pay the several thousand dollar balance in full. I opt to not change anything.

The next step is determining what I want it to say. Which font do I like? What color do I want the background? Which color granite do I want? Do I want any special emblem or symbols? I choose to keep the design simple, masculine, and classic. Something he would approve of.

Then we get to the part about my name. I originally ordered a stone large enough to put my name on should I decide to be buried with him. But I don't want my name on it right now in the event that I move, or get remarried, or just plain decide I don't want to be buried but rather cremated. There are so many contingencies to consider. More than once she says that it doesn't happen often that these contingencies have to be considered...she is a little befuddled at how to handle such a young widow. "Oh yes, I didn't think about that..." she says when I throw another hypothetical situation at her.

The plaque with my name must be ordered now- it is not an option to do it later. Though she is quick to reassure me that the plaque can be moved to a different stone should I be buried elsewhere or with someone else. I would just have to buy a new piece of granite to put it on. I am not happy about my name being on a grave stone at this age, but I acquiesce and agree to this.

The next step is to determine exactly how we want our names printed on the plaques. I choose full names- first, middle, and last. When we get to my name I stump her again. But what if I *do* get remarried? This plaque will say "Simmons"...she offers the suggestion of using my maiden name. No, that won't do. We talk some more about the options for all the contingencies that could befall me in the course of my life. I am one who always has a backup plan. Who always plans out all available courses of action in order to make the most rational decision. But I eventually realize that this is something that I will have to consider when the time comes as I cannot predict my future at this point. She asks for my date of birth. As she finishes writing, "July 23, 1980" she says to me, "You're too young." Yes, *this* I know.

If all goes well, I will have at least another 30 years ahead of me. Likely more. It is hard to fathom that I actually have more time ahead of me than behind me, and already I have essentially ended one chapter and am beginning a new one. Life as I knew it is over, and I am starting afresh. It is within the realm of possibility that I could be married to a new person longer than I have actually been alive up until this point. And yet, my name with my husband's surname will appear on a grave stone... waiting for me to die. It is mind boggling and surreal to consider.

My day will culminate in a visit from a guy I have been e-mailing and talking with for several weeks. He lives almost 300 miles away so we have only seen each other once before now. I am excited to see him again- to see if the connection we have established through conversation is as good in person. The last time I saw him went well, so I imagine this will too. We will spend the weekend going to dinner and concerts, meeting friends, maybe going to the lake, and getting to know each other better. I am happy about this development in my life. It brings me hope for my future. I know some will judge me and say I am moving on too soon. Or I am trying to distract myself from my grief, and there really is no way I could be ready. Some will judge him and wonder what in the world he could possibly see in a widow with young twins who lives 300 miles away. That's an awful lot of baggage for him to take on. But if I've learned anything in this process it is that there is no right or wrong way to do this. I can only proceed in ways that leave my heart and mind feeling content and at peace.

So while I started the day with a meeting to honor and celebrate the life of my husband, and followed it with a meeting to memorialize him forever, I will end the day with the opportunity to do something that helps me look towards the future. I have given up on always having a contingency plan. They never work out how I imagine them anyway. I am learning that the more I try to control my life, the more God shows me ways that I can't. He is the one who makes the plans.

So maybe, *just* maybe...
this new great guy who makes me happy,
is God's contingency plan...for me.

Tue May 31, 2011 | 08:36 PM |

Calendar

I'm a planner. Always organized with events on the calendar well in advance. At least I used to be. I'm not so good at it anymore. I always carry a calendar/planner in my purse. Today I took the 2010 planner out. I've stumbled across it several times since Andie died but always throw it back in. It's one of those little things I haven't wanted to face so I've just let it languish at the bottom of my purse for almost a year now- right next to the 2011 planner.

Today I took it out and thumbed through it. So strange to see remnants of a normal life documented. Doctor and hair appointments neatly penciled in. Vacations and days off of work. I was going through some health issues at the time and my doctors were playing around with my medications. Taking me on and off to see if my symptoms would subside. There are notes in this calendar about when to stop the medicine or start it again; comments about if my symptoms were getting worse or better so I would know what to tell the doctors when I went back in for a checkup.

I see the days where I circled the date four days in a row in a repetitive pattern and am reminded of how regimented the schedule can be when you are married to a cop. Andie's schedule was always rotating making it very difficult to plan things in advance. He worked 5 days on, 4 days off, another 5 on, another 4 off, then 6 days on followed by 4 days off. Then the whole cycle repeated again. I would go through the calendar months in advance and mark his rotation of days off so that when I was planning things I didn't have to sit and count the days over and over. I remember how irritated I would get when I would get off by a day and mess the whole pattern up, then I'd have to start from the beginning again to figure out where I went wrong. Grief is a lot like that...playing things over and over in your mind, going back to the beginning again to try and figure out where it all went wrong. Wondering where was the one moment that shifted everything in your universe? Only there are no erasure marks and do-overs with grief.

I look at the week he died. There is nothing there except the notation of when I started my menstrual cycle. We were on vacation when he died and I find it strange that I did not have the vacation written down. It's just a blank week on the calendar, as though nothing happened. As if it was just a boring, uneventful week in our lives. I keep looking and see that I had worked out his days off rotation until the beginning of August. Obviously planning for him to be around. Never imagining that I could stop caring what days he had off of work on June 18, 2010. The week after he died is completely blank too. Then the activity picks up again and there are meetings with lawyers, HR reps, insurance people, the funeral photographer, and a host of other things penciled in.

Dying is busy work for those left behind. The barrage of paperwork and decisions seems endless. Almost a year later and I'm still dealing with estate paperwork and final decisions on his headstone.

This planner is like a time capsule.
A glimpse into the mundane rhythm of life we had.
A written document that proves I had a normal existence once.
I consider throwing it away but instead decide to put in a drawer with the rest of the memorabilia that I have kept.
But for the life of me I can't think of a rational reason why...
It is just a calendar after all.

Thu Jun 2, 2011 | 02:21 PM |
Leap of faith...

"Sometimes you just have to take the leap and build your wings on the way down" - Unknown

There is a wonderful new blessing to my life. Someone who through fate, timing, answered prayers, or maybe just dumb luck eased his way into my life over the past couple of months. First through e-mails, then through texting, followed by phone calls and visits...never pushing past my comfort level. Letting me move at my own pace, but standing by all the while ready to walk this journey beside me. Allowing the connection to grow and evolve on its own. Slowing down to allow me to catch up if he got a step ahead of me. He has stepped aside to give me time and space as I need it...never selfish in his pursuit.

He is honest and respectful. Understanding and reassuring. Strong and confident. Gentle and kind. Caring and insightful. Interesting and intelligent. Protective and accepting. And above all, he is patient with me and this convoluted process.

He inspires, motivates, and challenges me to be a better person. He pushes me to let go and just trust in him, believe in the possibility of us, and have faith in God.

He is the answer to the repetitive prayer I've prayed: For God to allow my heart to be open, and accepting of whatever or whomever He puts in my path. For me to trust that if love walks into my life I can accept its presence with grace and dignity.

I have to admit that when I have heard stories of other widows who have moved on there was always a sense of judgment on my part. How could they move on so soon- how soon is too soon? How could they proclaim to still love their dead husband, but still have enough room in their heart to love another? I couldn't understand how that could even be possible. There was also a sense of jealousy that they had gotten lucky enough to find love again; I did not think that would ever be possible for me. But once you start down this road the issue becomes, how do you continue to hold the love in your heart for your husband while making room for new love to grow there too? I've found it's like having more than one child- your heart expands to fit the need. How do you incorporate who you were then, with who you are becoming? How do you integrate your old life with your new

169

life? I don't have the answers to these questions. These are still challenges I must face and I realize they will continue to be for some time…

I never imagined that I would be in the very position that I had scoffed at. I couldn't fathom that I could *ever* let go of my pain, or that I would ever even *want* to let go of the pain long enough to find happiness. After all, holding onto the pain has been all there was to hold on to. And I think that's why this worked. He eased his way into my life ever so gently that I didn't even know he was beginning to take up residence in my heart until it was too late to deny it.

I am on the precipice of something exciting and grand. I'm ready to take the leap of faith and see where I land and where this experience takes me. My perspective has shifted again and I find myself back in the place of believing that there is a power greater than us that guides us in the right direction even when the fog is too dense to see through it. I am acknowledging that I don't have all the answers to how my life is going to work out, nor am I supposed to.

I'm learning to enjoy it one moment at a time. To take things at face value without questioning or analyzing them to the point that I destroy them or push them away. I'm learning to let go. To surrender the control and accept that it's out of my hands…I'm learning to place the responsibility on the shoulders of someone much grander than I.

In my journey to find happiness…I am finding peace in my heart.

In my journey to find comfort…I am experiencing a calm stillness within.

In my journey to find love…I am opening my heart and allowing myself to take a risk.

Here I stand, humbly accepting that the universe indeed has more to offer me than I ever thought possible…

Sat Jun 4, 2011 | 08:19 PM |
Quiet mind...

"Go in all simplicity; do not be anxious to win a quiet mind, and it will be all the quieter. Do not examine so closely into the progress of your soul. Do not crave so much to be perfect, but let your spiritual life be formed by your duties, and by the actions which are called forth by circumstances. Do not take over much thought for tomorrow. God, who has led you safely on so far, will lead you on to the end." - Francis De Sales

I love this quote because now more than I ever I feel like my life and the decisions I have to make are the product of circumstance. This is certainly not how I planned my life. And it surely is not how I could've ever imagined it. But it *is* my life, the only one I have, so I must take it as it comes and make decisions based on the hand I've been dealt. And I *must* believe that God has a greater plan that I just can't understand at this point.

I know it will be a difficult process as I continue to walk the fine line between being excited about someone new, while still actively mourning the loss of Andie. I am not naïve enough to think that my grieving is done. I am not "over it" and I have not "moved on".

It has been a struggle to decide when I should let the world in on the fact that I am seeing someone. I didn't want to make the announcement too soon only to find that this relationship would fizzle out and I'd then have to face all the ensuing questions. I didn't want to keep it a secret as though it was something to be ashamed of, but at the same time I needed to feel secure before I announced such a momentous step.

And while I have had a couple of months to adjust to the idea and process my feelings about it, those who are just now learning of him are still shocked and surprised. Which only makes my comfort with it all the more awkward. I think they expect me to not be ready so soon, but I've done a lot of emotional leg work to get to this point. I've simply had a head start.

I am sensitive to the feelings of those who are still hurting, and who are not ready to see me "move on" with my life. I understand that Andie's family and close friends will have a harder time accepting this than my own family and friends. I know it will take time for people to get to a place of acceptance.

I know that people ultimately want me to be happy. Many have said as much to me on several occasions. In the weeks after his death people told me that it was okay to eventually move on. But saying that and actually being okay with it when it happens are two very different things. I think people have been okay with the *idea* of it, but when they actually see another man beside me they have almost a gut level reaction to it. I can see it in the subtle shifts of facial expression or body language. It seems that people are okay with the idea of it if it fits *their* version of how it should go and when, and not necessarily my version of it.

I have grappled with the idea of moving on for almost a year now. Mainly because people would often say to me that they knew I would find someone new one day. My own father in-law has had this discussion with me at least three times that I can remember. I almost felt a pressure about it in the early months after his death and it made me angry and indignant. But with time I have come to accept that this is in fact what I want for me and for my children. And it is also, I believe, something that Andie would want.

This is a hard position for me to be in. Wanting to be happy and being okay with this transition for myself, but also understanding that others are not yet ready for me to make this transition. However, what most people cannot even begin to fathom is the emotional work I have done to get to this point. It is I who has had to live every second of every day without him. I am the one who has two beautiful, yet constant reminders running around that look just like him, reminding me that he is not here. I am the one who remembers what it was like to have his face be the first thing I saw every morning, and the last thing I saw every night. Nobody else has had to deal with his absence on such a global level. Nobody else's life was changed with such magnitude. Most people get the emotional reprieve of going on about their own lives in their own schedule, which allows them to feel some normalcy. I have not had that luxury; nothing about my life has stayed the same. Nothing is as it was. And nothing feels normal. It has been a long, hard, process to get to this point.

He still consumes my thoughts for much of the day, albeit in a different way than before. Now it is often with fond memories. Sometimes I talk to him in my mind, imagining how he would guide me in daily decisions. It is rarely with pain that I remember him anymore. I would venture to say that to most people though, he is only a fleeting thought. He probably does not cross the minds of his friends daily anymore; only when something happens that triggers a memory for them. I can tell that me and the girls are not on people's minds as much by the drastic slow down in contact from others checking on us. And this is okay. It means that everyone is healing, and everyone is moving on...just at a different pace.

The bottom line is that I have to do what feels right in my heart. What makes me happy, content, and fulfilled. I have to move on with my life in a way that gives me a quiet mind. Worrying about what other people think of my actions only increases my anxiety and apprehension. And letting go of the control feels so freeing. This is a new part of me that has emerged through this experience. A more mature part of me, and I like it. I don't have to control everything in my life, and I don't have to have it all planned out. Controlling comes from a place of fear. I don't want to live my life in fear. I want to appreciate what I have while it's here instead of always planning for the worst case scenario.

The circumstances of my life have drastically altered who I am, who I want to be, and where I want my life to go. I am giving it all up to God with faith that he will lead me in the right direction in the end.

Mon Jun 6, 2011 | 08:54 PM |
Punch drunk...

"There are people who make things happen, people who watch things happen, and people who don't know what the hell happened." - Unknown

Usually I'm one who makes things happen. Today, I don't know what the hell happened.

It really all started yesterday evening. Maybe it was because I had been with the girls all weekend and was feeling worn out. They had been sick and had grossness coming out both ends for three days straight. More likely, it was grief that I have put on the back burner letting me know that it has not forgotten about me, though I would like to forget about it.

Yesterday I started having a feeling of dread come over me. Not sadness or despair or anger. Not loathing or melancholy. Just dread. I couldn't really pinpoint what it was all about until tonight.

A series of small setbacks happened today that under normal circumstances would've been easy to deal with. But today for some reason they all seemed overwhelming and insurmountable, and underneath it all was a sense of dread. As is my usual custom, when I start feeling deep emotions I turn inward and pull away from others. The new guy noticed right away- long before I even acknowledged to myself that something was going on. As is normally the case with a new relationship we went down a path of wrong assumptions and miscommunications. I continued to pull inward instead of just saying what was on my mind, which is that the one year anniversary is around the corner and I flat out don't want to deal with it. I feel like I need 6 more months if I'm being honest- this year has gone by so very fast.

He felt more and more edged out and didn't know why. I was trying to spare his feelings and not harp on my issues over my dead husband. Which only backfired, leaving him feeling left out and me feeling confused about how my consideration for his feelings was the wrong thing to do. Sometimes I feel like the deck is stacked against us; we are in a new relationship at the hard part where you are learning each other's idiosyncrasies and communications styles, then add to that the fact that we live 300 miles away and only see each other occasionally (not exactly how a normal relationship develops), then top it off with the grief monster. So while all of this was rolling around in my overly analytical and apprehensive brain, I got a call from my mom. She's been having hip pain that won't go away. She was on her way to get an x-ray today since the medication they've given her hasn't helped. I got off the phone with her and immediately went into doom and gloom panic mode. I was sure she had bone cancer and was going to die. I was even picturing how the phone call would go in which she would tell me that things looked bad. *Crazy*, I know. She called me when it was done and said they want to do an MRI to look more closely but it does not appear to be anything serious, or at least life-threatening. Then some irritating things happened at work that only added to my work load, and bothered me on a level it never would've if I wasn't already worked up.

So there I sat trying to finish up my work for the school year, ruminating on where I went wrong with the new guy (despite the fact that we had managed to get back on the same page), if my mom was going to die, and how I was *ever* going to finish the work I should be focusing on when they just added to my plate. And down the spiral went...dread was closing in big time.

The kicker of the day was that I had to leave work and go straight to a meeting to finalize plans for the 5k in honor of Andie. Ever since yesterday when this first started creeping into my psyche, all I can think is "Why did I sign up for this?" And that's where the dread started. I'm feeling like I don't want a yearly reminder that requires months of planning ahead of time...I've worked myself into a situation that will require that I devote a couple of months a year before the anniversary to thinking about him. I should've left well enough alone and just had to deal with the *one* day of the anniversary. Way to go, overachiever! Lately I've had the overwhelming sense that I just want to move on. I want to shut the door on this old life in a way and start over. I want to run away from the pain. Not very brave of me, and not very strong- but it's the honest truth. I'm just so tired of having *his* death be the focus of *my* life. It feels so heavy all of the time and I want to cast it off.

I walked in the door 11 hours after leaving my house this morning feeling drained, obliterated, and incoherent. I felt emotionally exhausted and couldn't really do more than sit on the porch in a stupor while the girls played.

And that's when all of this finally came together in a flash of insight. I finally saw how I got from point A yesterday evening: dread. To point B tonight: punch drunk*.

Maybe I can sleep it off...

*punch-drunk
adj.
1. Showing signs of brain damage caused by repeated blows to the head. Used especially of a boxer.
2. Behaving in a bewildered, confused, or dazed manner.

Sun Jun 12, 2011 | 03:23 PM |
Brace for impact...

"Peace: It does not mean to be in a place where there is no noise, trouble, or hard work. It means to be in the midst of those things and still be calm in your heart."

This time next week will be a hard day. All the pomp and circumstance of the one year anniversary the day before will be over. Just like after the hustle and bustle of funeral arrangements end and you manage to survive the actual day of the funeral it is the day after, when the quiet ensues that the let down of emotion begins to surround you. If I steel myself for it and brace for impact, then maybe it won't wipe me out so hard...or maybe it will.

When I reflect on this past year I am amazed at how fast it has gone. I think because most of it was spent in a stupor and I didn't really even realize days were going by for so long...it's like the first 6 months were a blur, then I woke up and the last 6 months have crept by. Or maybe it was the other way around. Maybe it all crept by, day by day, in the beginning and lately time has sped up. I've come so incredibly far, yet still have so very far to go. I think about the coming months and all the "big" dates that will be fast approaching. The ones that did not even register on my radar last year because I was still in shock. My birthday, the girls' birthday, our wedding anniversary, the holiday season...they will feel different this year, I know. The sting will be stronger because the numbing anesthetic of shock has worn off.

Though this year will be harder, there is also so much more to look forward to. There are so many things on the horizon for me that give me something to hope for. This time last year my outlook was so bleak- I did not think I would ever find any joy in anything ever again. I am especially grateful for some of the friendships that have deepened through this experience. I feel so supported and loved by such a great group of friends who have unconditionally supported me in my pursuit of hope and healing.

This coming week feels heavy and overwhelming. I'll be busy all week with last minute plans and tasks to help get the 5k run in honor of Andie off the ground- we will run on the one year anniversary. There has been a lot of focus on all the details over the past few weeks and it's been weighing on my mind heavily. I'm also meeting with the home builders this week to go over the first round of plans for the house. I'm still not sure I can afford to build it on my own so that's part of the discussion we'll have. But I'm excited about the prospect of having a project to look forward to, and for the opportunity to literally "rebuild" a life for me and the girls somewhere.

I was supposed to go out of town to visit the new guy this past weekend to give me a small mental break before this week wiped me out. Plans changed quickly though when he called and said he had an impromptu job interview down here and would be coming my direction instead. He interviewed on Thursday and we spent the weekend together. If he gets this job and moves to this area it will push our relationship to a different level. One in which we can actually see if this could work in a real world sort of way instead of just weekend visits every now and then. I'm excited about it. But it's also a lot to take in and consider, given the timing of it all.

He is supposed to know by midweek if he got the job or not. I must also approve the final sketch of Andie's headstone this week. Almost a year to the day of laying him in the ground, I will finally approve what will mark his presence there forever. There's a lot of weight in that decision and it's not something I'm looking forward to. And, as if all of that wasn't enough, I'm starting the girls in daycare this week for the first time ever. I'm so excited that they are growing up into sweet little girls, but this huge milestone also reminds me they are not babies anymore. I am so sad about how fast they are changing and growing. I want to hold onto these sweet years with them, it is hard for me to even remember what they were like a year ago...not even walking or talking. They are the starkest reminder to me of how much time has passed and the fact that life keeps moving whether you want it to or not. Might as well get on board and enjoy the ride.

As the year anniversary draws near I think of how most of the world wants to you to be pretty much done with the grieving process by now. One year seems to be the universal marker of healing. Most other people have moved on in their lives and they realize that certain days will still be hard for you, but for the most part they don't want you to wallow anymore. They don't want to keep hearing about your dead spouse or how hard your life is. This is when people start pushing you to be happy again, or get out and do things, to move on already. They don't realize how much of your life and your major life decisions are still impacted by the loss of the person who used to help you make those decisions; or how much you still miss sharing with that person on a daily basis. Then there are those who believe you are moving on too fast, taking on too much, or who just aren't ready to move on themselves so they are hurt by the pace you've set.

Those of us who grieve know that the timeline is arbitrary. It is personal to each of us and fluid in its movement. Some days we are ready to shut the door on the old life and embrace the new. Other days we want to go back in time and stay stuck in the memories of the past, hoping that somehow we can just wake up from this bad dream. We feel pulled between two worlds, stuck in the middle never knowing which direction is the right way to go. There is no right way, of course. You just have to go with your gut and hope that it's the right decision for the time. And that's what I'm doing. I'm not sure if I'll build a new house, or manage a brand new relationship well, or ever be okay with the fact that the girls are continuing to grow and becoming farther and farther from the babies they were when he died...but I do know that I feel a peace in my heart about all of my decisions.

I know this next year will be hard.
I know there will be struggles and difficult decisions to make along the way.
I know my children will always serve as a vivid timeline for me, how each day we all get a little bit farther away from him.
But all I know to do is keep moving, keep striving for better, keep praying,
And of course...keep pushing.

Mon Jun 13, 2011 | 08:37 PM |
Feel better...

The weight of this week is bearing down on me. I am irritable and lack patience with the girls today because I am stressed and worried about all the things I need to accomplish this week. I try to remain calm with them but am appalled at my own behavior and how quickly I get angry at them for minor things. How many times can you tell a toddler "no" before they finally get it? I have come to the realization recently that I *can't* do this alone anymore, and do it well. I don't *want* to do this alone anymore. I don't want to be a single parent. I'm tired of it. I don't want the girls to be raised in a single parent household. I cannot be a good mother to them without help, as hard as that is for me to admit. I need a co-parent, a partner, a support system that doesn't come and go a couple of nights a week. I need someone who will have my back and be there to emotionally support me, so that I can be healthy enough to emotionally support my children. It's not fair to them that I am tired and overwhelmed most of the time because they end up bearing the brunt of it. This, I am not okay with. Paradoxically, I find myself behaving in some of the ways that I used to get angry with Andie for when he lost his patience. Funny how that happens isn't it? I guess when you are left to take on the role of both parents you step right into those shoes...no matter how uncomfortable they may be. Because you don't know any other way to do it, really.

I just want to feel better.
About my life.
About my parenting.
About my future and theirs.
About myself.

"Just Feel Better" by Aerosmith and Santana

She said I feel stranded
And I can't tell anymore
If I'm coming or I'm going
It's not how I planned it
I got a key to the door
But it just won't open
I know I know I know
Part of me says let it go
That life happens for a reason
I don't I don't I don't
Because it never worked before

But this time
This time
I'm gonna try anything to just feel better
Tell me what to do
You know I can't see through the haze around me
And I'd do anything to just feel better
I can't find my way
God I need a change
And I'd do anything to just feel better
Any little thing to just feel better
She said I need you to hold me
I'm a little far from the shore and I'm afraid of sinking
You're the only one who knows me and who doesn't ignore that
my soul is weeping
I know I know I know
Part of me says let it go
Everything must have its season
'round and 'round it goes
Every day's the one before
But this time
This time
I'm gonna try anything to just feel better
Tell me what to do
You know I can't see through the haze around me
And I'd do anything to just feel better
I can't find my way
God I need a change
And I'd do anything to just feel better
Any little thing to just feel better
I'm tired of holding on
To all the things I leave behind
It's really getting old yeah
I think I need a little help this time
I'm gonna try anything to just feel better
Tell me what to do
You know I can't see through the haze around me
And I'd do anything to just feel better
I can't find my way
God I need a change

And I'd do anything to just feel better
Any little thing to just feel better

Transitions...

This is such a time of transition in our household...changes are happening all the time.

The girls attended their first day of daycare yesterday and did wonderfully, though the morning routine was a little rough on Allie. Addie was very excited to go and thrilled about her new big girl lunch box. Allie wanted nothing to do with any of my best attempts at getting her excited about going. Addie tried to reassure her and make her feel better by giving her hugs and kisses, and then headed for the door eager to get in the car. Allie proceeded to throw her lunch box and pitch a fit. We managed to get to daycare and they only cried for about 15 minutes after I left and of course when I arrived to pick them up 7 hours later they weren't even excited to see me because they were having so much fun. I have to admit that I had envisioned the movie scene where the kids coming running across the playground and leap into your arms because they've missed you so bad. I barely got a nod and smile when I walked up before they went back to playing. All in all, I'm happy that this was not a difficult transition for them...or for me.

For a year now I have visited his grave every month and marked the time by how much grass had grown over the dirt patch. I had it in my mind that when the grass was completely filled in, and there was no longer any sign of the earth being ravaged, that *then* it might actually seem real. While the dirt was still fresh I just could not wrap my mind around the fact that he was in the ground...and this is still a hard concept to grasp. Yesterday afternoon I gave the final approval on Andie's headstone. It will be here in several weeks and is so symbolic of the finality of his death, and of this year. Seeing it there will serve as a reminder that this all really *did* happen.

The school year has finally come to an end and as of yesterday I'm officially finished with work for the year. I tend to measure my years by the school year rather than a calendar year as many who work in schools do, and being that Andie passed away this week last year it only deepens the feeling that "this past year" is coming to a close. I always welcome the summer when I can mentally put away all the stresses of the previous school year and start fresh in a couple of months. I especially feel this way now. I am looking forward to a summer this year with hope and excitement of having some time to enjoy with those I love. I want to savor all the good times and continue to strengthen the bonds I've developed with new and old friends. My relationships with others are so much more important to me now and I don't want to take them for granted.

So much has changed in the past year and there are so many new things on the horizon for us. New adventures and experiences for us all. New relationships are starting, and old ones are evolving. Most of them in good ways, with a deeper bond and appreciation for those around me ever present on my mind. I have a renewed focus on doing what is right for me and the girls and reprioritizing so that it fits our needs, not what I think everyone else wants. This has been the hardest year of my life but it has brought me some perspective and maturity.
I'm looking forward to all the new transitions we have headed our way. I feel positive about our future for the first time in a while. I am ready to start the rest of my life with a new focus.

As they say...
The only thing that stays the same is...
Everything changes.

Sat Jun 18, 2011 | 08:16 PM |
At a loss...

365 days have passed. For the first time in a long time I feel at a loss for words. This day is not what I expected it to be. It did not feel heavy and dark as I anticipated. Strangely, it has felt almost like any other day in this journey. Just another 24 hour period to get through. Just another succession of steps- one foot in front of the other.

The first post I did after Andie died still seems appropriate after a whole year has passed...

Originally posted 09/5/10:

"So it's been a while since my last post. You've probably noticed a lot has changed on my blog. Well, that's because a lot has changed in my life. Andie passed away on June 18, 2010 and left me with two beautiful daughters to raise. It's taken me a few months to feel like I have my feet back on the ground and even that seems only momentary.

I considered not blogging anymore but have decided that it's a good way for everyone to keep up with how me and the girls are doing- I know you're all wondering. Raising twins is hard, but raising twins as a single parent is TOUGH- and humbling.

I've learned a lot about myself in the past few months. I've had to ask for help more than I'm comfortable with, I've had to compromise on a lot of things, and I've had to adjust my life plan. I've learned that I have more love and support than I ever knew was possible, but I've also learned that all of that seems inconsequential when you've lost your other half. I've learned that grieving for your spouse is just a small piece of the picture. You also grieve the loss of who you were as a wife, the loss of your hopes and dreams, the loss of the future you had planned, and most of all you grieve for your children and how they will never know and experience their dad as you did.

People often ask how I am doing. The truth is: it depends on the moment, the day, the hour, what song is on the radio, what street I'm driving on, or who's asking. I'm doing as well as I can with what I've been given.
My girls are my saving grace and keep me looking forward to the next moment, day, or hour..."

Mon Jun 20, 2011 | 08:21 PM |

Heavy...

I felt like I was on an upswing for a while but something washed over me today. Things were getting better, but as is the case with grief, it comes in waves. You can only ride the crest so long before it crumples beneath you.

There is a new relationship to look forward to, new hope for the future. Maybe, just maybe, the girls and I will have a complete family someday. Or maybe not; I feel so uncertain. Relationships are hard. They take a lot of work. I'm not sure if I have the emotional strength and fortitude to devote to it as this great man deserves; I'm not sure I believe in myself and my abilities to cope anymore. I feel weak and doubt myself. I don't want to give up on the hope of happiness. I'm just feeling like I'm not good enough to make it through the tough stuff. I'm feeling overwhelmed with single parenthood. I'm feeling tired of spending the evenings in silence because there is no one to here to talk to. I'm tired of feeling needy and desperate for attention and reassurance. I'm tired of worrying about what the rest of the world thinks and trying to please others, or grieve the "right" way in the "right" time. I feel indignant that this is the hand I've been dealt. I feel guilty that I did not have the guts to visit the cemetery on the one year anniversary, nor on father's day; back to back days that were just too much. Will he think I'm a coward? Will he think I have moved on past the point of caring? Is he even there?

I feel dark, despondent, and discouraged....

185

I just want it all to get better now.
I've made it through a year.
When is enough, enough?
Grief feels so heavy tonight.

Tue Jun 28, 2011 | 02:49 PM |
It's over...

"It isn't for the moment you are struck that you need courage, but for the long uphill climb back to sanity and faith and security." - Anne Morrow Lindbergh

After a lot of heartache and much discussion, the new guy and I are over. Our life circumstances were just too much to overcome. He lives close to 300 miles away and it would be a year before he could even entertain the idea of moving. We would have to maintain a difficult long distance relationship that would be very expensive with the amount of travel required to see each other. We both have children who are our first priorities, and leaving his daughter isn't an option. Uprooting mine right now to move to be with him is also not an option. Not to mention, there is a lot of emotional baggage to deal with on both sides of the table when there is a widow involved. He had his own emotions, thoughts, and feelings regarding my widowhood and where he fit into the equation. And I have mine. Navigating all of this just became too much. The hardest part to accept is that we were really great together. It's hard for two people who want desperately to be together to call it quits... to let something so wonderful go when you know that if the circumstances were just a little different you could be great together. Luckily the split was amicable with no hard feelings on either side, and we will maintain a friendly relationship. Maybe we'll be lucky enough to have our paths cross again someday under different circumstances.

Though the relationship was short-lived it taught me a lot. It was the push I needed to prove to myself that I want to live again and to love again. It taught me that I want to be adored and cherished by someone. I want to be that very special something to someone. It taught me that my heart really is open to receiving joy. I loved being married and I love being in relationships- I crave emotional intimacy with another. I want to be married again. I love the security of being with one person.

It was so nice to be appreciated and admired again. It was great to have someone enjoy my children and be around to help me with them. It was nice to have a shoulder to lean on and an open ear. It was wonderful to have a man make me feel gorgeous and great just the way I am. He motivated and challenged me to be a better person in so many ways. We seemed so perfect for each other; we connected intellectually, spiritually, and emotionally. We had great chemistry- people who saw us together could tell we had a true, genuine affection and love for each other. He is a phenomenal man who set the bar very high. I'm afraid that nobody will be able to measure up and be as patient, mature, and understanding as he was. I have a hard time believing that any other man would be so willing to take on the difficulties of a widow with young twins and do it with the strength he did.

I am saddened that we couldn't find a way to make it work. My evenings will once again be very lonely with no one to look forward to talking on the phone with. No one to text me during the day just cause they're thinking about me. The loss of comfort and companionship will reopen some of the wounds of grief that were not yet healed. A risk I knew I was taking when I entered into the relationship...but knowing you could get hurt doesn't make it hurt any less.

I will always remember this relationship with fondness.
I will always remember him with admiration.
When I started this relationship I was constantly nervous because it all seemed too good to be true.
I just wish I hadn't been right...

Thu Jun 30, 2011 | 03:09 PM |
Purging...

I started cleaning out his closet a few days ago. I have felt the need to clean out closets, get rid of clutter, and re-organize my life. Get rid of all that is unnecessary and get back to simple. It feels almost like nesting, only I'm not nurturing a new life within me- I'm trying to create a new life around me. I finally finished his closet today.

Neatly sorted boxes of things I will keep and things I will give away. It is amazing how much one person accumulates during a lifetime. I'm astonished that there are five large boxes of clothes to give away, and only one box that holds the clothes I feel so strongly connected to that I want to fold them reverently and stack them gently as though *they* could be hurt in this process.

I was rather detached while doing it. They are just shirts, and pants, and belts, and ties...but I cry openly when I come across the t-shirt he wore the day the girls were born. Their tiny sets of footprints stamped on his chest in black ink after the nurse finished doing the same on their birth certificates. It was one of the happiest days of his life, and had you told us then that 10 months later he would be gone...

Out with the old, in with the new.
Purging.
Lots of purging...

Wed Jul 6, 2011 | 08:24 AM |
Heartache...

The girls have been particularly interested in Andie's picture again lately. I find them often standing near it. Talking to the picture, gesturing, waving, carrying it around, kissing it...

I watch how they interact with the men in their lives. Their grandfather, uncle, male friends of mine, even how they were with the new guy. They love to curl up and cuddle with a big guy, they love to horseplay and be silly with a man, they crave the kind of interaction with a male that I can't provide.

It will only be another year or so before they realize they don't have a father and the questions will start.

My heart hurts for that day...

Mon Jul 25, 2011 | 02:19 PM |
Voice...

I have lost my voice.

My writing voice.

I have not posted in a while because I cannot wrap my mind around how to explain the place I'm in. There is a lot going on that I'm not sure should be shared with the world. There are good things happening, sad things, angering things, exciting things, and even some scary and anxiety-provoking things.

There are things I literally cannot write about- expressly forbidden actually. There are things I want to write about, but out of respect for those involved will not. And there are things I simply am choosing not to write about to protect myself...I need to not be so bare to the world right now.

I'm not sure if I will ever come back to writing like I used to. It served a wonderful purpose in allowing me to cathartically release my grief and emotions for a long time. But I don't know if that is necessary any more.

Maybe my voice will find its way back to me in time...

{PART FIVE}

ALIVE...

He heals the brokenhearted and binds up their wounds.
Psalm 147:3 ESV

Sat Jul 30, 2011 |10:19 PM |

Alone...

24 hours have passed in which I have been 100% completely and utterly alone.

My children are away with their grandparents for the weekend. My mom is out of town. My best friend is doing her own thing.

I have not been alone and by myself for more than a few hours in well over a year. There is always someone here to keep me company, distract me, entertain me, check up on me, or rely on me for something.

I have been anxious and terrified to spend this time alone. I have dreaded it for days...but now that it is here I realize I am surviving it. Just like I have survived every other moment for the past year. The anticipation of this has proved worse than the actual experience of it, which is usually the case.

I have had moments of feeling lonely, but more than anything I feel triumphant.

One more thing that I have done, and done *alone*.

Literally.

Sat Oct 01, 2011 | 08:38 AM |

Think less...

I decided to sell Andie's truck since it has been sitting in my driveway for over a year and is rarely used. His cousin came down from Oklahoma to purchase it this week.

Yesterday I was running errands around town when I pulled up to a stop light. At the light perpendicular to me was Andie's cousin driving Andie's truck. It caught my eye from a distance and my breath caught...as I got closer and realized it really *was* his truck the tears immediately began to fall. Seeing his truck out of context like that was almost like seeing a ghost. I was wiping away tears before I even realized I was crying. Before I even had a chance to try and stop them...

It's funny how a deep emotional reaction always happens at least a split second before your rational brain can process it. One of the reasons it's so hard for people to hide their true emotions I suppose...the facial expressions of pain and anger that flash across the face a second before we can compose ourselves is almost always a dead giveaway.

This makes me think of how whenever I ask the girls to apologize to one another for something, they never actually use any words despite the fact that they can talk. They always choose to give each other a hug and kiss as a way to say they are sorry. They actually *feel* it rather than just think it and say it. They're still innocent enough to be okay with processing emotions instead of shutting them down like adults do.

Maybe they're on to something there.

Maybe the emotional center of the brain that short circuits the rational mind is programmed that way for a reason.

Maybe we all need to allow ourselves to feel more...and think less.

Tue Oct 25, 2011 | 11:16 AM |
Catch...

Most days are good. Most days are filled with joy and laughter with the girls. Andie still crosses my mind every single day, and it is usually with fondness that I remember him. I still talk to him every night before I go to sleep. But there are still moments that cause my breath to catch and hot tears to well up in my eyes.

Like when the girls brought home artwork from school when they were learning about families. Little balloons on construction paper. Each balloon labeled, "Mommy", "Daddy", "Addison", and "Allison". I see the word "Daddy" and debate in my head whether it is more appropriate for them to have given him a place in their artwork or not...I decide in the end that I'm glad he was included.

Or like the moment in church this week when I had to take a few deep breaths to hold back the tears because all of a sudden memories of us sitting in the pew whispering and snickering to each other like children came flooding back...

Or watching the girls play in the bathtub and realizing that he never got a chance to see their beautiful, playful personalities start to emerge...

Or the moment two nights ago when my wedding ring sitting on the bathroom counter caught my eye. I was compelled to put it on again to remind myself what my hand used to look like with it on...it felt so heavy. I didn't remember it being so heavy.

Or even as I sit and type all of this and acknowledge to myself that the pain is still in fact, very much there, and very much real.

These are the kind of moments where just for a second the world stops again.

Where I am thrown back into a kind of surreal existence in which I have to make myself believe again that it all *really* happened.

These are the kind of moments that cause my breath to catch...

Fri Dec 30, 2011 | 04:05 PM |
New Year...

This time last year I was dreading the arrival of a new year. I did not want 2010 to end, as it was the last year that my husband was alive and somehow the calendar change felt like closing one more door on my old life. I wasn't ready to exist in a year in which he never would.

This year I'm not minding the thought of starting a new year. I have a pretty fresh perspective on things. I'm learning that I like the new "me" that has emerged since his death. I'm more assertive in speaking up for my own needs. I communicate much better...If I think it, I say it. I don't put as much stock in what other people think of me, and am living more authentically *for me*. I value the people in my life even more than before. Strangely, I even have less anxiety about the future on most days. I still have moments where I want to control everything and plan out how the next five years will go, but on most days I'm at peace with not knowing what the future holds. I've finally accepted that even if I plan it...it usually doesn't happen that way. I've allowed God into my life even more and my faith has continually been strengthened. I focus more on having fun and enjoying what I have while I'm here instead of looking for things that need improvement or change. I still think of Andie every day and talk to him every night before I fall asleep. He shows me he's here less and less through signs, but I know that's because he knows I need to move on. Though, I don't doubt that he's still very close by protecting the three of us. I've been involved in a very special relationship for a few months and it feels comfortable and peaceful to have someone in my life again. It feels good. And it feels right.

My girls are shining beacons of hope for the future. They grow and change every day and remind me that life is not stagnant. It keeps going whether we want it to or not.

This year, I'm happy to be along for the ride.

Wed Jan 11, 2012 | 11:30 AM |
Fill the hole...

I'm halfway through the second year. I still can't believe that much time has passed already. They say the second year is harder and in some ways I completely agree. There are still so many little things that are like a slap in the face and remind me that the life I had is gone.

The other day I was filling out some paperwork and the marital status section didn't have "widow" as an option. I used to hate checking the widow box, but this time I felt incensed that I didn't get the choice. I am not married. I am not single. I am not divorced. I do not identify with any of these, and I felt irritated that "half of me was unexpectedly stripped away without my consent" wasn't an option. So I scrawled "widow" in and moved on.

I also had to fill out some medical information sheets for the girls. I got to the parent information section and under "father" I write "deceased". The next half of the page remaining blank because I do not need to fill in his address, contact information, insurance data, place of employment, or any other mundane detail about him that no longer exists. The blank page staring back at me is like a metaphor for my life...everything is going just fine and then there's a big blank spot all of a sudden where he is *just* not there anymore. Like the moments when the girls do something remarkable or funny and I think, "Andie needs to see this," but of course he doesn't because he's just not there.

I got my yearly renewal policy for my home owner's and auto insurance in the mail. I open it and see that they hadn't dropped his name off of the documents even though I called them months ago to rectify this situation. I call and re-explain that he died and it is *just* me now. They are embarrassed for the mistake and offer condolences. I find myself trying to make the lady on the phone feel better because she feels so bad. This happens often...I find myself saying in these situations, "No *really*, it's okay."

I get some form in the mail from Social Security that wants me to document how I've spent the benefits I receive for the girls. Frankly, I feel it's none of their business. Parents receiving child support don't have to answer to anyone regarding how they spend their money...why does the government have the right to pry into my life in such a manner? The money he earned and contributed to Social Security is rightfully mine to do what I want with it... though of course if they *must* know, I spend it on exorbitant child care costs consisting of both daycare *and* a nanny in the mornings to get the girls off to school because I can't manage to do the carpool by myself and still get to work on time. I spend it on food, clothing, medical care, and shelter for my children- things they need to survive. I spend it on family vacations in the hopes that I can create some happy childhood memories for them. I spend it on maintaining some semblance of a normal life for them.

I struggle with this hole in my life, this absence of him, this blank page to fill. On one hand I'm sick of having these little moments keep bubbling up to remind me of what I've been through. But on the other hand I don't want the alternative, which is to fill the spot, to check a different box, to let go...

The dilemma of wanting my children to experience a family unit and have a father figure versus wanting to eternally preserve this sacred spot for him and not allow someone else to fill that role is almost a constant struggle. It's hard to let my guard down and imagine that I could love someone like that again and run the risk of going through all of this for a second time...

But I'm learning to let someone new in, and each day a piece of that wall comes down and I see the hope and joy of what it could be like to actually fill the hole...

Thu Jan 12, 2012 | 03:54 PM |
Co-parenting?!?!?

The daycare called me today and said they wanted to run an idea by me. They wanted to see how I felt about separating the girls and allowing Addie to move up to the next class. She is now potty-trained, and developmentally and cognitively ready to be challenged a bit more. Allie is not yet potty-trained (one of the requirements to move up), and her language is still a tad bit behind Addie's so she's not quite ready. I obviously have mixed feelings about this. It's a BIG decision in the twin world; whether or not to separate the kids, and especially when they are this young.

Later in the day, I ran all this by "the boyfriend" (sounds so silly at this age to say boyfriend). He listens as I explain what the daycare told me and then is silent. "Do you have an opinion?" I ask. "Yes." he replies. I wait through a long pause before saying, "*Well*, are you gonna share it with me?" He smiles and begins to talk. We discuss the topic, both offering opinions on the matter, discussing the pros and cons for each girl, and come to the conclusion that I should let Addie move up. It's not fair to hold her back from progress just to be with Allie, and furthermore, Allie can move up as soon as she's potty-trained. Plus it may afford them some independence and help them not be so nitpicky with each other in the evenings if they haven't spent the entire day together at school.

As he and I are discussing this, a HUGE realization hits me...actually several realizations hit me.

1. The first being that it is so surreal to be talking to another man about my children as though they are his. Asking for his input and advice as though we are co-parenting. Actually it's weird to be talking to anyone about major parenting decisions. My normal course of action is to make the decision myself then talk it over with those I trust to see if they agree...*never* have I done the reverse to try to come to a joint conclusion. I never got

the opportunity to discuss a parenting dilemma with Andie- he was gone before any major decisions had to be made for them.

2. I realize that I have made a HUGE step in the trust department if I was actually willing to let my guard down and consult him in this manner instead of doing it all by myself as a single parent. It was such a relief to include someone else in the decision making instead of shouldering the pressure and burden alone. More and more I realize I am letting him into my private world and it actually feels good. I *want* to share the load with someone. I'm really comfortable with it. And so is he.

I share all of this with him...that I think it is a big step for me to include him in this discussion rather than just make the decision myself, as it shows that I am opening up and trusting more....he says he knows this already which is why he chose not to offer his opinion in the beginning until I specifically asked him for it.

That's when the next realization hits me...

3. This guy *really* gets me and understands how I tick. He knows me *so* well that he knew he couldn't cross that boundary with me until I offered the invitation. He respects the limits I have and doesn't push me outside my comfort zone. He just supports me where I am at the moment.

That is a level of trust, communication, and respect that I am proud to have in my life, and excited to have in my relationship. I then realize...this one's going to be a keeper.

Wed Jan 18, 2012 |12:31 PM |
Throw momma from the train...

Last night I freaked out. Totally overboard, off my rocker, freaked out. I've been in this relationship for about four months. Long enough for us to discuss the future and see ourselves together in it. Long enough for it to be (in my crazy head) time

to be making out a timeline of when things might happen. I
don't do well with unknowns. I think this is something a lot of
widows struggle with, especially when the loss was sudden and
felt out of our control. We want to control everything else so we
don't ever have to be blindsided again. But, I readily
acknowledge that this is also just part of who I am at the core. I
like plans. And goals. And knowing what's around the bend and
what I'm up against. The problem is that there are a lot of
uncertainties in both of our lives right now that can't be rushed.
And it's not that I want to rush it. It's just that I want to know a
general idea of how it might all play out.

This stems from my insecurity, and fear of loss and
abandonment, I know. I worry about letting my guard down,
giving someone my heart, and possibly getting hurt again or God
forbid, going through loss again. Some days it seems it would be
easier to stick to what I've got. It's not the most fulfilling, but at
least it's what I know and I'm comfortable with it. I've spent 19
months doing it my way, on my own, without anybody else's
input. It's hard to think about letting someone else in on the
routine, into my space, into my head, and mostly into my heart.
Relationships of course take lots of compromise and I haven't
had to compromise for quite a while. Change brings
disequilibrium. I want my equilibrium back.

So I started freaking out. Maybe this really *isn't* what I want. Or
maybe I want to rush it too fast and jump into something before
I've given it due time- I worry this will scare him away. What if
I'm making a huge mistake? What if we disappoint each other
and get hurt in the process? What if, what if, what if...

I feel like I'm on a train that's headed to a great destination. Or
so I *think*. The problem is I can't see what's around the bend. I
can't tell if we're going to crash and I'm going to get hurt. So
maybe I should just jump. But that'll hurt too...so I have to
hedge my bets. I'll definitely get hurt if I bail out now and lose
such a great man. And I *might* get hurt if we go around the bend
and there's an obstacle in the tracks. Maybe if I continue to be
this difficult, and overanalyze and worry too much about things

that are out of my control it's going to push him away and he'll actually end up *throwing* me from the train. Or maybe, with a stroke of luck I'll round the bend and utopia will be waiting for me. Only time will tell. A concept I despise.

When I share all of this with him he is the epitomy of perfect. He listens, reassures, empathizes, and validates. I'll spare you the "he said", "she said" of it all, but I will tell you that after he hears my neurotic and over-analytical musings, he says something to me that strikes me deep inside. He saw right through me and called me on it. Not in a bad way, in a way that showed me that he understands how my mind works maybe as well as I do. He's only known me four short months and already understands how I think, how I feel, and how I process, in ways that only my best friend understands. He's got an intuitive sense about what I need from him on an emotional level and isn't afraid to provide it. He *truly* gets me in a way that nobody ever has and it shocked me. My normal course of action would be to dodge and weave when I feel like someone's seen all my cards, to divert the attention to something else. But all I could do was acknowledge that he was right. That he hit it square on. And it felt *so* good to let someone see me for me, and know they still accept me that way.

So when I tell him that I feel like jumping from the train and calling it quits to save us both pain down the road, he says he's not letting me jump.

He's holding on tight and going to keep me safe.

And the cool thing is...I actually believe him.

Mon Jan 23, 2012 | 12:15 PM |
Take a step...

"We must be willing to let go of the life we had planned, so as to have the life that is waiting for us." – Joseph Campbell

This process is a constant struggle of moving forward and letting go. And in the moments where I'm forced to recognize that I have to let go a little bit more I get scared and emotional.

I can't believe that it was almost two years ago already that Andie and I bought the land to build our dream house on. And almost a year ago that I did the consultation with the builder about how to site the house and what trees to clear off the land. A year ago I thought I was ready to jump in full force and build the house. But after that consultation I got scared again because moving forward and building the house we had planned without him felt like too much to take on by myself at the time. So I put the project on hold for a while.

But I'm feeling the itch again...there is so much I've had to let go of since he died. I've let go of the title of "wife" and given up the idea of having more children. I've lost the dream of reaching a 50th wedding anniversary with someone and traveling to all the destinations we said we'd go to for each decade we made it through. I've had to let go of the life we worked hard to establish, the friends we had as a couple, the dreams we had together. I've had to rebuild a new circle of friends, a new way of life as a single parent, and I've had to create my own dreams about how my future will look without him in it. And every step of it has been painful and heartbreaking.

But the house is the one last thing we had together that I just can't let go of. I want to build the house to fulfill something we had. I want to build it as a way to honor him, to acknowledge that while my life has to go on without him, there are still parts of him and what we had that I don't have to give up. Moving on doesn't have to mean letting go of everything. And it doesn't mean forgetting him. I think that's what I've been afraid of. That if I move on his memory and his legacy will be forgotten over time. I don't want him to just fade away.

I've struggled with how to keep him as a part of my daily life while building a new normal for me and the girls. I still think of him throughout the day, and most nights I talk to him before I say my prayers and fall asleep. And what I'm realizing is that I *can* mesh the life I had with the one I want to create. I don't have to give up one to have the other. And more importantly, I can do all of this at whatever pace *I* want to set. If I wait until I'm "done" grieving I'll never move forward. Because the truth is, I'll never be done and it's not fair to me or the girls for me to stay stuck in this place of pain just because I'm scared.

So I'm going to move forward in the direction of building *our* house. Only, I'm going to have to do it by myself.

I just have to take the first step...

Tue Jan 24, 2012 | 08:37 AM |
Opening back up...

I am writing again these days and it feels good. It's almost like exercising after a long break. It hurts to do it but you know you should, and when you're done you feel proud, and lighter, and better for it.

I took some time off because frankly I was tired of grieving. Tired of hurting. Tired of exposing my inner most thoughts and feelings to the world. I quit reading other widow blogs for a while too. Staying connected to this circle of loss felt too heavy and depressing. I needed to nurse my own wounds for a while and protect myself after having been so exposed for so long. I needed to focus on happy things and moving forward. I needed to force myself to have some fun and look towards the future. And I did those things, I continue to do those things, but I still continue to grieve as well.

So I'm back now. Back to writing. Back to following others. Back to processing some of which I purposely avoided for a while. I usually am not inspired to write unless it comes from a place of pain, anxiety, or the need to process the many sides of grief. I find that coming back to this circle is like a warm blanket. I read other blogs and again am wrapped in the comfort of relating to their words. I am cocooned in safety because there is, in fact, someone else out there who I can relate to. I find that writing and sharing in this format is cathartic and healing.

A lot has happened over the past few months in which I have chosen not to share every detail of my life as I once did before. I have found that some things are worth protecting and keeping private. But I'm ready to let you all in again on how my life is shaping up, and more importantly I'm ready to open myself up to the support you all give me.

The journey of grief never ends, and as my life continues on I find it only gets more interesting and complicated. Each new step I take in moving forward has to be reconciled with the person I used to be and the life I used to have. The struggles now are not so much about accepting that he is gone, (I get that part. I live every day without his presence.) but about accepting that he won't ever be here again, which actually are two very different things.

Thu Feb 02, 2012 | 01:08 PM|
Push me...

This is hard
This is hard
This is hard

This seems to be the refrain running through my mind most of the time these days. Aspects of my grief are being brought out daily as each day is a new experience with someone new, and I am constantly reconciling the new with the old. Constantly readjusting my focus. Constantly experiencing happiness and joy with the underlying tinge of sadness that this isn't really how it was all supposed to turn out. The tears come so easy these days. Quick and hot on my cheeks. I am not the tough, strong girl I used to be. I allow myself to be more in touch with my emotions these days but it hurts. I question whether I am really ready to be in another relationship yet if I feel so emotional about all of this. But the answer is that you're never really ready- no matter when it happens all of these issues will bubble up and you have to endure to move past it.

I thought I had gotten to a place of calm functioning with my grief. I was not doubled over in pain every day anymore. I could make it several days in a row, sometimes weeks without crying. So to have it all brought back out and on the surface again feels doubly painful and confusing. How could something that makes me so happy bring me so much heartache? All I can think is...

No, I'm not going back here.
I was past this.
I don't want to feel this again.

But I have to. You cannot know how grief will color and overshadow everything you do for the rest of your life until you walk into each and every new experience. You cannot prepare yourself for how it will feel to fall in love with someone else until it starts happening. And it hurts because you grieve all over again for the loss of the one you once loved. You can't begin to understand how it will feel to have another person literally in his place at the table, sitting beside you in church, and holding the children, until you see it happening.

Being with someone new and trying to put all of my trust in him to be there for me only reignites my abandonment issues. The two most important men in my life both died suddenly and unexpectedly... my father when I was 15, and fifteen years later it was my husband. The fear of that kind of loss happening again is paralyzing. I simply could not manage to pick myself back up from that kind of devastation.

I don't want to revisit the pain so it seems easier to run from it. I think about sabotaging what I have in this new relationship and I even give it a pretty good effort, but in the end I can't bring myself to walk away from this incredible man who is so amazingly understanding of it all. A man who wants to help me heal and wants to be beside me in the process to support me through it. And as he reminds me, I could put this off but inevitably I will be with someone someday and all of this will come out again. Pay now or pay later.

So in pushing him away I'm really acting out of self-preservation, but in doing so then I stay stuck. This is when I need someone to push me. To be behind me and say it's all going to be okay and I will survive this. And he does. He does so with such dignity and gentle encouragement that I can't help but believe him.

So I'll continue to let him push me.
But damn it hurts.

Fri Feb 03, 2012 | 04:00 PM |
Live for now

"The secret of health for both mind and body is not to mourn for the past, worry about the future, or anticipate troubles, but the live in the present moment wisely and earnestly."
- Buddha

One thing I am grateful for in this process of loss is how it has forced me to discover the real me. It has forced me to understand that life is fleeting and I want to enjoy the rest of mine as much as possible. I want to feel alive and excited about my future. It has forced me to see that spontaneity and having fun is actually okay, I don't have to carefully and meticulously plan my life so as to always be the "responsible" one. It has shown me that it's okay to make mistakes, it's okay to do things my way and not care so much about what others think, and it's okay to take risks. I've learned so much about myself in the past year and a half. Grief has taught me to take an honest look at who I am and what I believe in. It has made me more aware of what is truly important to me.

Not long after Andie died I briefly but seriously considered packing up and moving to Costa Rica for a year. I had the sudden urge to flee everything I had ever known and start over. I wanted to not take one more minute for granted and wanted to take advantage of every opportunity to do something fun, and exhilarating, and crazy.

Well, while I am not moving to Costa Rica permanently, I have rented a house there for a month this summer. I want my girls to have fun childhood memories to look back on. I want them to remember their mother as someone who enjoyed life, and *really* lived. I have made a promise to myself that every summer we will travel somewhere fun, and exciting, and to a place where they can learn about the world and a different culture.

I've also decided to get a tattoo. Something Andie would totally be against. But that's okay, because I've decided to get the tattoo for *me*. I haven't completely decided on the design yet but it will be something in honor of him. It will incorporate my mantra "Push" to remind to always keep pushing.

Keep pushing the boundaries of my comfort level.
Keep pushing myself to grow as a person.
Keep pushing myself to move forward and live authentically for me.

Just keep pushing...

THE REST OF THE STORY

Obviously there is not really an end to my story. My healing continues, as do my struggles to overcome what life has thrown at me. I continue to find joy, excitement, and hope in the future. Just as I continue to be brought to my knees with pain and despair when the grief is unforeseen and inescapable.

I've come to understand that I can accept what I've been given as a second chance. An opportunity to start over and live boldly and authentically. Something many do not ever have the opportunity to do. I recognize now, that while his loss has been one of the most devastating and debilitating events of my life, it also has taught me some beautiful lessons. I now have a fresh perspective on who I want to be, how I want to live, and who I want to share it with. Through the struggle to heal my priorities have become clear.

My journey to redefine myself doesn't end here. I will always keep striving for better, keep acknowledging my blessings, and of course, I will always keep pushing...

Join us as the story continues to unfold at
http://2peasinthepod.blogspot.com

For everything there is a season, and a time for every matter under heaven: a time to be born, and a time to die; a time to plant, and a time to pluck up what is planted; a time to kill, and a time to heal; a time to break down, and a time to build up.
Ecclesiastes 3:1-3 ESV

ABOUT THE AUTHOR

Brooke Simmons currently resides in the Hill Country in central Texas. She continues to raise the twins with the loving support of her close family and friends. She is a Licensed Specialist in School Psychology by trade and a writer by accident. She enjoys the laughter of her children, the joy of new experiences with those she loves, and the warmth of the Texas sunshine on her shoulders. Find her at http://2peasinthepod.blogspot.com